Jesus
In the
Bible

Jesus
In the
Bible

KENNETH BOA

THOMAS NELSON PUBLISHERS®
Nashville
A division of Thomas Nelson, Inc.
www.thomasnelson.com

The author is grateful to Rev. Greg Asimakoupoulos for his collaboration and editorial help in developing the content for this book.

Published by Thomas Nelson, Inc., P.O. Box 141000, Nashville, Tennessee, 37214.

Scripture taken from *The Holy Bible,* New King James Version (NKJV). Copyright © 1979, 1980, 1982 by Thomas Nelson, Inc. Used by permission. All rights reserved.

Produced with the assistance of The Livingstone Corporation. Project staff includes Paige Drygas and Greg Asimakoupoulos.

Printed in the United States of America

ISBN 0-7852-4874-9

Library of Congress Cataloging-in-Publication Data is available.

02 03 04 05 06 — 6 5 4 3 2 1

Contents

Introduction

The Bible . . .

It has been printed and distributed more than any other book ever. It is far and away the best-selling book in history. The Bible is, arguably, the most beloved book of all time—and probably the most hated, too.

No other published work has ever had such a profound global influence. History shows that the truths of this remarkable book have not only transformed individual lives but also entire cultures. In its breathtaking power and haunting beauty, the Bible is unique. It is like nothing else in the entire world.

And yet the Bible remains a great mystery. Despite the fact that most homes have at least one copy, many people wonder, *But what is the Bible, really? What is it about? What does it say? What does it mean?* And most significantly, *How are its claims relevant to my life today?*

Sadly, to many, the Bible is a kind of *Christian's Almanac*—an odd hodge-podge of religious trivia, hard-to-understand laws, and unbelievable miracles.

To others, God's Word is viewed as a kind of disorganized, ancient, two-part scrapbook. The first half (the Old Testament) features the Jewish people; the second section (the New Testament) focuses on the Christian church. The result of this is mild curiosity, not wonder and awe. As long as such thinking dominates, the Bible will be seen as an interesting relic and maybe a nice thing to have around, but not _the_ great Story of the universe that gives ultimate meaning to one's individual life.

Thus my goal for this little book: To help you see that the Bible—though made up of sixty-six books written by some forty different authors over roughly fifteen hundred years—_is_ a single story. It is, in fact, _God's_ story—a breathtaking record of the Creator's dealings with His creatures.

Moreover, I want you to see that the dominant character in this divine plot is none other than Jesus Christ. Contrary to what many believe, Jesus wasn't a last-minute afterthought in God's eternal plan. He doesn't just show up suddenly on page 983 as plan B (or plan G!) in God's feverish attempt to save sinners. On the contrary, Christ is the focal point of the entire Bible—from beginning to end. He's the one to whom the whole Old Testament points, the one on whom the Gospels focus, the one at whom the rest of the New Testament looks back.

Believe it or not, Christ permeates the Scriptures. He is the living Word (John 1:1) of whom the written Word speaks constantly. Everywhere we read, we find hints, glimpses, foreshadowings, veiled references, graphic pictures, whispered allusions, and prophetic mentions of Jesus. He moves through all the pages of the Bible, not just in the Gospels or in the apostles' epistles. Look carefully, and you will see Him again and again in the poets and prophets.

A few years ago a publisher came out with a wildly popular series of children's books featuring a tall, bespectacled traveler in a striped shirt and a red hat named Waldo. Every page in these books featured a highly detailed picture of some famous event or popular place. Millions of children (and parents) carefully studied these busy drawings asking repeatedly, "Where's Waldo?" Why? Because somewhere in the midst of all that clutter, Waldo could be found . . . if you only looked long and hard enough.

That's the basic idea behind this book. It is an attempt to help you find Christ throughout the Scriptures. I'm convinced that once you do, you'll gain a better and deeper appreciation for God's immeasurable love for you, and you'll catch a glimpse of His marvelous plans for your life. You'll see how your story is a part of God's larger story. And your life will never be the same.

Kenneth Boa
June 2002

Jesus

In the

Old Testament

CHAPTER ONE

Jesus in the Books of Moses

Some fourteen centuries before God gave the world a *living* revelation of Himself through the person of Jesus Christ, the Creator began giving *written* revelations of Himself to an aged man named Moses. Many scholars believe this took place during Israel's forty years of wilderness wandering, the period after God had delivered them from Egyptian bondage and before they settled in the Promised Land.

No one knows exactly how all this transpired. But somehow, as Moses lingered in the presence of the living God—whether on Mt. Sinai, in his own tent, or in Israel's traveling worship center called the Tabernacle—God spoke and Moses wrote. The inspired result of this divine–human collaboration is the first five books of the Bible, sometimes called the Torah, the Pentateuch, the Books of the Law, or simply the Books of Moses.

If there were a contest for "The Best-Known Section of the Bible," this five-book collection might very well win. Genesis and Exodus contain hugely famous events. The stories of Creation, the disaster in the Garden of Eden, the great Flood, the parting of the Red Sea, and the giving of the Ten Commandments are universal accounts that get lots of press.

The main plot of the Bible is God's cosmic plan to recapture the glory He deserves and to rescue the creatures He loves by sending Jesus Christ. The main character of the Bible is Christ.

Who hasn't heard of Adam and Eve, Noah, Abraham, or Moses? Every few years, even secular Hollywood feels compelled to take yet another stab at a cinematic retelling of one or more of these old, familiar stories from the Bible.

But, as noted in the introduction, we must be careful not to get so caught up in the exciting subplots of the Bible that we miss the main plot— God's cosmic plan to recapture the glory He deserves and to rescue the creatures He loves by sending Jesus Christ. The main character of the Bible is Christ. In the words of the apostle Paul, "He is before all things, and in Him all things consist" (Colossians 1:17). If this statement is true (and it is), then Christ is the underlying presence who gives coherence to the entire story of the Bible.

Genesis

Genesis is Moses' first book, the book of beginnings. The first two chapters describe the beginning of the universe and the beginning of the human race. Adam and Eve, the first couple, are the pinnacle of God's work, crafted in His very image (1:26) to live in fellowship with God and to reflect His glory. But this spectacular plan is quickly attacked. In chapter three of Genesis, we also see the beginning of the spiritual disease called sin. Adam and Eve listen to the tempting voice of the serpent, doubt the goodness of their Creator, reject God's authority, and declare their independence. While these actions are catastrophic, they do not catch God by surprise. Immediately, the all-knowing and all-powerful Creator enacts His eternal plan to rescue His rebellious human creatures.

Though the word is not used until much later in Scripture, God begins hinting at a *Messiah,* a Savior sent from heaven who will undo the terrible effects of Adam's choices. As Genesis unfolds, this Deliverer, whom we know as Christ, is said to somehow be the offspring of Eve (3:15). He will come, ultimately, from the line of Seth (4:25). He will be the son of

Shem (9:27), the descendant of Abraham (12:3), of Isaac (21:12), of Jacob (25:23), and a member of the tribe of Judah (49:10).

Not only does Genesis contain these direct yet subtle references to Christ, but it also gives us fascinating glimpses of Jesus through assorted people and events of Genesis. Scholars and theologians call these pictures that point to something or someone in the future *types*. Literally, a type is a historical fact that illustrates a spiritual truth.

> *A type is a historical fact that illustrates a spiritual truth.*

According to the New Testament, Adam is "a type of Him who was to come" (Romans 5:14). In other words, Adam's life in some ways points vividly to Jesus. Consider that both individuals entered the world through a special act of God, as sinless men. But while Adam is the head of the old creation, Christ is the head of a new creation.

There are several other compelling types of Christ in Genesis. Abel's acceptable offering of a blood sacrifice alludes to Christ, and there is a dark parallel between Abel's murder by Cain and Christ's murder by His Jewish brethren.

Melchizedek (whose name literally means "Righteous King") is a strange and shadowy figure who suddenly appears in Genesis 14. He is the king of Salem (which means "Peace") who brings forth bread and wine and announces himself as the priest of the Most High God. He blesses Abraham and receives a tithe from him. Some scholars believe that this one who was, in the words of Hebrews 7:3, "made like the Son of God," was in fact Christ Himself. Christ, after all, is known as the Prince of Peace (Isaiah 9:6).

Joseph (ch. 39—50) is yet another type of Christ. His character and experiences foreshadow the coming of the Messiah in that both Joseph and Christ are objects of special love by their fathers, both are hated by their brothers, both are rejected as rulers over their brothers, both are conspired against and sold for silver, both are condemned though innocent, and both are raised from humiliation to glory by the power of God.

Exodus

The second book of the Pentateuch is Exodus. It is usually at this point that many well-intentioned Christians abandon their annual attempt to read through the whole Bible. While Exodus begins with a series of jaw-dropping miracles and the giving of the law at Sinai, the book ends with long chapters of detailed instructions regarding the construction of the Tabernacle, Israel's portable house of worship. The tendency, if we are not careful, is to regard Exodus as a book of ancient religious anecdotes and trivia, unrelated to modern Christianity.

But as we look closer, we see that Christ figures prominently in the Bible's second book. Exodus contains no direct messianic prophecies, but it is full of types and portraits of Christ.

Christ can be seen first of all in Moses. In numerous ways, Moses is a type of Christ (Deuteronomy 18:15). Both Moses and Christ are prophets, priests, and kings. (Although Moses was never officially made king, he functioned as the ruler of Israel.) Both are kinsman-redeemers (that is, they intervene to save those to whom they are related). Both are endangered in infancy and must be hidden by their parents to escape death. Both voluntarily renounce power and wealth in order to associate with those they seek to save. Both are deliverers, lawgivers, and mediators. Coincidence . . . or divine plan?

Christ is clearly seen in the solemn Jewish Passover—that historic event (ch. 12—13) that required the blood of a pure, sacrificial lamb to be painted over the doorways of the Israelites' homes to spare them from God's judgment and then usher them to freedom. John 1:29, 36 and 1 Corinthians 5:7 make it clear that Christ is our Passover Lamb. It is His death, His blood applied, as it were, over the doorways of our lives, which rescues us from divine condemnation.

The Exodus itself illustrates Christ's work on our behalf. In the New Testament, the apostle Paul relates baptism to the Exodus event, for passing through the water symbolizes death to the old life and identification with a new way of living (Romans 6:2–3; 1 Corinthians 10:1–2).

On the other side of the Red Sea, we see God's preservation of His people in the wilderness, miraculously supplying them with manna (the bread from heaven) and water (ch. 15—18). What many Christians do not realize or tend to forget is that the New Testament applies both of these situations to Christ (John 6:31–35, 48–63; 1 Corinthians 10:3–4)! These Old Testament events depicted the coming of Christ—the true Bread of Life, the Living Water who alone can quench one's spiritual thirst forever.

Most Christians are startled to discover all these hints of Jesus in the Book of Exodus. Yet there are even more. The feasts prescribed for Israel in Exodus

23:14–19 (and described more fully in Leviticus, the third of Moses' books) all point to Christ. Each of these annual celebrations portrays some aspect of His ministry. The Passover lays the foundation for the substitutionary death of the Lamb of God. The New Testament records that Christ died on the day of Passover! The Feast of Unleavened Bread illustrates the holy walk expected of the follower of Jesus (1 Corinthians 5:6–8). The Feast of Firstfruits foreshadows Christ's Resurrection as the firstfruits of the resurrection of all believers (1 Corinthians 15:20–23). Christ rose on the Day of the Firstfruits. The Feast of Pentecost speaks of the descent of the Holy Spirit after Christ's Ascension. The Feast of Trumpets, the Day of Atonement, and the Feast of Tabernacles connect to events associated with the second advent of Christ. This may explain why these three are separated by a long gap from the first four in Israel's annual cycle.

And then we come across those chapters in Exodus devoted to the plans for the Tabernacle. Many Christians read these chapters, roll their eyes, and shut their Bibles. Or they doggedly plow ahead, wondering why in the world God inspired Moses to include such a mountain of detail. I admit, on a superficial level, this section first reads like a contractor's memo. But look again. Realize that in its materials, colors, furniture, and arrangement, the Tabernacle is a picture of perfection in God's eyes, showing us that there is only one, perfect way we can be made right with God, through Jesus Christ His Son. The development plans begin with suffering, blood, and death and progress to beauty, holiness, and the glory of God. The tabernacle is Christian theology in a physical form!

Lastly, the Book of Exodus introduces us to Israel's priesthood (ch. 28—29). More than just costumed religious figures, these individuals in their character, dress, and conduct were intended by God to foreshadow the ministry of Christ, our great High Priest (Hebrews 4:14–16; 9:11–12, 24–28). Jesus made the final sacrifice that put an end to sin forever and made us acceptable to God. Every mention of an Old Testament priest should prompt us to think of Jesus and His ministry on our behalf.

Leviticus

Leviticus is baffling to most Christians. It is a bloody book, filled with sacrifices and ancient, often hard-to-understand rituals. The temptation, again, is to skim these pages and to shake our heads at the strange religious beliefs of the ancient Jews. If we do, we miss so much. If we are careless here, we miss Jesus.

The fact is that Leviticus is replete with types and allusions to the person and work of Jesus Christ. The five offerings described in chapters 1—7 all point to Christ. Compare the descriptions found here with the picture of Christ found in the Gospels, and the connections become crystal clear. The burnt offering typifies Christ's total offering in submission to His Father's will. The meal offering typifies Christ's sinless service. The peace offering alludes to the fellowship that believers have with God through the work of the Cross. The sin offering typifies Christ as our guilt-bearer. The trespass offering pictures Christ's payment for the damage of sin.

Only when we see Leviticus for what it is—a manual or guidebook for how sinful people can approach a holy God—can we fully appreciate its message. Only when we imagine ourselves living under such a system for centuries can we begin to sense how thrilled the disciples must have been when John the Baptist pointed at Jesus of Nazareth and exclaimed, "Behold! The Lamb of God who takes away the sins of the world!" (John 1:29).

Leviticus points vividly to Jesus. He alone is the spotless Lamb who can make an eternal and final payment for sin. He alone is the perfect High Priest who can represent human rebels before the holy Judge of the universe.

Numbers

Numbers documents the sad story of Israel's unbelief. God had delivered His people from Egyptian bondage and promised them the land of Canaan. But when they refused to trust and obey God and take the land, they were consigned to wander in the desert for forty years. A trip that should have taken two weeks took an entire generation. If you can imagine spending four decades doing little besides going to funerals, then you have a sense of the high price of their disbelief.

Did God abandon His people during this dark time? Not at all. God sustained them and blessed them with His presence, even in their chastening. And as with all the other books of Moses, we find glimpses of Christ in Numbers. Perhaps the clearest portrait is the incident of the bronze serpent on a stake. Numbers 21 records that a number of Israelites were bitten by snakes in the desert. God instructed

Moses to fashion a bronze serpent on a pole and lift it high. All who looked at the serpent in faith recovered (21:4–9). Here we have a stunning picture of the Crucifixion. "And as Moses lifted up the serpent in the wilderness, even so must the Son of Man be lifted up" (John 3:14).

Another type of Christ in Numbers was the desert rock that miraculously poured out water to quench the thirst of the multitudes. Referring to this event, the apostle Paul wrote, "They drank of that spiritual Rock that followed them, and that Rock was Christ" (1 Corinthians 10:4). The miracle of the manna, provided faithfully for that entire forty-year period, also pictures Jesus, the self-described "Bread of Life," who came down from heaven centuries later (John 6:31–33).

At one point in Numbers, the ungodly prophet Balaam exclaims, "I see Him, but not now; I behold Him, but not near; A Star shall come out of Jacob; A Scepter shall rise out of Israel, And batter the brow of Moab, And destroy all the sons of tumult" (24:17). To what was he referring? He was foreseeing the coming kingdom of God's Messiah.

We could also mention how the pillar of cloud and fire that guided the people of God in those wilderness years signifies Christ's guidance and presence with His people today. Or we could note how the sinner's refuge in Christ is seen in the establishment of six cities of refuge. We could talk about the red heifer sacrifice described in Numbers 19 and what it symbolizes. But by now, I bet you can guess. These events, too, point to Jesus.

> *Christ is the star of God's drama. He is the central character, the protagonist, the hero.*

Need we say it again? Christ is the star of God's drama. He is the central character, the protagonist, the hero. From beginning to end, the books of Moses are all about Christ.

Deuteronomy

The most obvious reference to Christ in Deuteronomy is found in 18:15: "The Lord your God will raise up for you a Prophet like me from your midst, from your brethren. Him you shall hear." (See also 18:16–19; Acts 7:37.) Moses spoke these words in his final address to the children of Israel.

How was Moses a type of Christ? Again, he was the only biblical figure other than Christ to fill the three offices of prophet (34:10–12), priest (Exodus

32:31–35), and king. (Although Moses was not tech-nically a king, he essentially functioned as ruler of Israel; see 33:4–5.) Both Moses and Christ were in danger of death during childhood. Both were saviors and intercessors. Both were rejected by their brethren.

At the end of the Book of Deuteronomy, God calls Moses home—but not before working through this extraordinary man to give the world, through his life and through his writings, a remarkable glimpse of Jesus, the coming Messiah.

Can you see Him? Look closely. There He is, again and again—Christ, appearing all over the pages of the first five books of the Bible.

CHAPTER TWO

Jesus in the Historical Books

Joshua

Once Moses died, his pen and parchment were passed on. Others would be required to chronicle the colorful history of God's chosen people. Joshua was the first to pick up where his mentor had left off. His book describes the critical lessons Israel learned under his command while waging war against surrounding nations. Although their enemies were larger and stronger, Israel learned that ultimate victory comes from faith and obedience.

Although there are no specific prophecies of Jesus in this book, Joshua himself is an obvious representation of the coming Savior. His name, which means "Yahweh is Salvation," is the Hebrew equivalent of "Jesus" (a Greek name). As Joshua leads the nation of Israel across the Jordan River into their promised inheritance, he foreshadows the One who will bring "many sons to glory" (Hebrews 2:10). The apostle Paul recalls Joshua's role when he writes,

"Now thanks be to God who always leads us in triumph in Christ" (2 Corinthians 2:14).

The baton of succession was passed to Joshua so that the victory line Moses had failed to reach would eventually be crossed. What Moses set in motion (but failed to achieve) is at last accomplished. This is a graphic picture of Jesus' succession of the Mosaic Law. His sinless life and unjust death resulted in a victory over sin that Moses could not reach (John 1:17; Romans 8:2–4; Galatians 3:23–25; Hebrews 7:18–19).

The blood-colored cord that Rahab hung from her window to guarantee deliverance from the advancing troops is a sure sign of the salvation from future judgment that Jesus' blood provides.

But Joshua gives us more than shadowy images of the future. When Joshua encounters "the commander of the army of the Lord" outside the walls of Jericho (5:13–15), he is actually in the presence of a pre-incarnate appearance of Jesus. Though it sounds strange, it's true. Why else would Joshua fall down and worship Him? Why else would he be instructed to take off his sandals like Moses did at the burning bush in the presence of the Lord? Why else would

Joshua refer to Him as his Lord (Exodus 3:2; Joshua 5:15)?

When Joshua sent two spies into Jericho prior to Israel's invasion, a prostitute by the name of Rahab provided them secret shelter. To show their thanks, the spies promised her family would not be attacked if she displayed a scarlet cord in her window to set her home apart (2:17–20). The blood-colored cord that Rahab hung from her window to guarantee deliverance from the advancing troops is a sure sign of the salvation from future judgment that Jesus' blood provides.

Judges

In stark contrast to the Book of Joshua, Judges does not offer a complimentary picture of God's people. Instead of obedient men and women conquering a land by trusting God's power, we see an idolatrous nation disobeying God and tasting continual defeat. But thankfully, this book also provides a glimpse of what Jesus would do for all of us who, like the ancient Jews, struggle with disobedience. Each one of the seventeen judges is a kind of "savior." (Fourteen are listed in Judges and three more in 1 Samuel.) They rule with a hand on the gavel and an eye toward

God. Thus, like Jesus, they provide spiritual direction and restore the guilty into fellowship with God. Also like Jesus they invite those for whom they came to follow them (Judges 3:28; Mark 1:17).

The individuals the Lord chose as judges were accustomed to wearing "hats" that fit their particular style of leadership.

The individuals the Lord chose as judges were accustomed to wearing "hats" that fit their particular style of leadership. Some warrior-rulers (like Othniel and Gideon) were quite comfortable wearing a crown. Eli was at home with the priest's cap. And Samuel and Deborah were definitely fitted for a prophet's turban. Curiously, these three different approaches to "judging" provide a cumulative picture of the three offices Jesus held (prophet, priest, and king). What the judges strived to achieve as mere humans, Jesus accomplished with perfection.

Ruth

Following Judges we are introduced to the delightful story of Ruth. It's a real-life, romantic tale starring a gracious Moabite woman. Ruth is widowed at a young age and courageously opts to leave her homeland and move to Israel with her mother-in-law, Naomi. Not only does Ruth end up marrying Boaz (an Israelite of influence), but her grandson David also becomes Israel's greatest king (and the earthly ancestor of Jesus).

In this short book the Hebrew word *goel* is used thirteen times. It means "close relative" (3:9) and conveys the concept of kinsman-redeemer. That's exactly who Jesus turned out to be for the human race—one of us who became the advocate for all of us. According to ancient Hebrew law, the goel must fulfill certain requirements in order to qualify as a redeemer. And the requirements anticipate what Jesus Himself did for us.

For one thing he must be a relative of those he redeems (Deuteronomy 25:5, 7–10; John 1:14; Romans 1:3; Philippians 2:5–8; Hebrews 2:14–15). This family member must also be able to pay the price of redemption (2:1; 1 Peter 1:18–19). In addition he has to be willing to redeem the individual who is about to be claimed by another (3:11; Matthew 20:28; John 10:15, 18; Hebrews 10:7). One final requirement is that the kinsman-redeemer must himself be free and not in debt. Boaz qualified in a financial sense. Jesus did in a spiritual sense. Because He was sinless, He was free from the curse of sin. The kinsman-redeemer is a clear picture of the role Jesus would play for us.

1 Samuel

In the first of two books that bear his name, Samuel shows us how the people of God transitioned from a leadership characterized by judges to a system of divinely appointed kings anointed by God's prophets. Because he is himself a prophet, priest and judge, Samuel embodies the roles that Jesus will later fulfill. Much like the one of whom he is a type, Samuel is highly revered by those over whom he rules as he ushers in a new age.

For Samuel, the new age consisted of King David's reign. Not only was David Israel's greatest king, but as a "man after God's own heart," his awareness of God also influenced the collective heart of the nation. For Jesus, whom Scripture refers to as "the Son of David" (because of His earthly lineage), the new age is a time of restored fellowship with our Creator.

1 Samuel focuses on the life of David and reveals details that definitely point to the One who would be called by his name. Like Jesus, David is born in the sleepy little village of Bethlehem. His reputation as a shepherd is validated by his years with his fa-

ther's flocks. This lowly shepherd becomes the king of the Jews. He is the anointed king who becomes the forerunner of the messianic king. Through years of struggle and danger David tastes the kind of rejection Jesus would fully digest. Many of his psalms reveal his firsthand experience of being forsaken. (See Psalm 22; Matthew 27:46.)

> *Through years of struggle and danger David tastes the kind of rejection Jesus would fully digest.*

David is the most famous of Jesus' earthly ancestors in the long and distinguished messianic line. In addition to being referred to as the "Son of David" (Luke 18:38), Jesus is called "the seed of David according to the flesh" (Romans 1:3) and "the Root and the Offspring of David" (Revelation 22:16).

2 Samuel

As we move to the prophet Samuel's second volume, aspects of the life of David that foreshadow the ministry of Jesus aren't as focused. But they are just as common. This is a book that records both the highlights and lowlights of this celebrated king's reign. In chapters 1—10, David's life is a far better portrayal of the future Messiah than is the case in chapters 11—24.

And that's because the pattern of David's sinful choices mars his potential.

Still, in spite of his sins of adultery, murder, and deceit, David remains a man after God's own heart. This is seen in his response and faithful attitude toward God. He is a true servant of Yahweh in the way he rules as monarch. Like Jesus, David characterizes his reign with justice, wisdom, integrity, courage, and compassion. His throne is none other than the one that belonged to Melchizedek (the Righteous King; see Genesis 14:18). David is the standard by which all subsequent kings are measured. Does the term "king of all kings" sound familiar?

Although David barely compares to the One who holds a scepter seated at the right hand of God's throne, he comes closer than anyone else in Scripture. In 2 Samuel, God makes a covenant with David (7:4–17). Without understanding the magnitude of it, the shepherd-turned-king receives God's three-fold promise of an eternal kingdom, throne, and seed. Amazingly, these are the same three promises given to Jesus (Luke 1:32–33).

It's no small wonder the son of Mary and Joseph is called "the son of David" (Matthew 21:9; 22:42) who would sit on the throne of David (Isaiah 9:7; Luke

1:32). And on a curious note, David ruled for a time in Hebron before the thirty-three years he reigned in Jerusalem. Jesus' life on earth as king of the Jews was also for thirty-three years, but this was only a continuation of His majestic rule in heaven that preceded His Incarnation.

1 Kings

As one king's reign gives way to the one who succeeds him, so the history of the former is put on the shelf while a new one is written. And thus we are introduced to a new book. The first half of 1 Kings traces the rule of Solomon, David's crowned prince. He succeeds in constructing the temple in Jerusalem while extending the boundaries and glory of the nation to an unsurpassed level. Solomon's fame and respect is celebrated throughout the known world and anticipates the unequaled glory the Prince of Peace will claim one day (4:34; Philippians 2:10).

Solomon's wealth, honor, and majesty bring about knowledge, peace, and worship in Israel. But the primary cause of Solomon's international reputation is his fabled wisdom. His proverbs contained in our Bible are only a few drops from God's reservoir of truth.

But they illustrate how practical truth becomes when it is clothed in memorable phrases.

Although he was not all that intelligent morally, his mind-boggling wisdom points ahead to the one the apostle Paul would call the "wisdom of God" (1 Corinthians 1:30). He really does characterize the "desire of the ages." Yet in spite of Solomon's wisdom, splendor, and influence, when Jesus comes onto the scene and announces His arrival, it is only fitting that He say "indeed greater than Solomon is here" (Matthew 12:42).

Although he was not all that intelligent morally, his mind-boggling wisdom points ahead to the one the apostle Paul would call the "wisdom of God."

But Solomon is not the only messianic prototype in 1 Kings. Later in the book we are introduced to Elijah (18:1). It is true that he actually resembles John the Baptist more than Jesus, but his prophetic ministry punctuated with miracles also hints at Him, too.

2 Kings

In the ongoing saga of Israel's history, the monarchs' game of musical chairs would be humorous if it weren't so tragic. Second Kings chronicles the collision course toward captivity on which both the northern and southern kingdoms are headed. We are witnesses to Israel's (the Northern Kingdom's) inability to sustain a stable government. Nineteen evil kings (comprising nine different dynasties) lead the people far from God. But in Judah (the Southern Kingdom), a single dynasty preserves the line from which the promised Messiah will come. From an earthly point of view, Jesus is able to trace His branch on the family tree to the trunk of David and the tribe of Judah (Matthew 1:1–16).

From an earthly point of view, Jesus is able to trace His branch on the family tree to the trunk of David and the tribe of Judah.

As mentioned previously, Elijah pointed to Jesus but was a clearer forerunner of John the Baptist (Matthew 11:14; 17:10; Luke 1:17). But it's the younger man for whom Elijah prepared the way, Elisha, who definitely reminds us of Jesus. When you stop and think about it, the similarities are impressive. Elijah (like the Baptist) lived apart from people, stressed the law, judgment, and repentance. But Elisha, (like Jesus) lived among the people and emphasized grace, life, and hope. (See 4:8–37; 6:14–23; 8:7–15; 19:16–21).

1 Chronicles

Let's hear it for repetition! Every good teacher knows students are more apt to grasp the facts if they are exposed to them more than once. In the Book of 1 Chronicles we peek again at the Jewish history found in 2 Samuel and 1 Kings. But it's not exactly a repeat. In addition to a review of the material already covered, the writer provides a color commentary of the events from God's perspective.

As in 1 and 2 Samuel, Jesus is foreshadowed in this book through the life and influence of King David. Just as before, God's covenant to David is a prelude to what the Messiah will bring about (7:11–14). Some might try to reason that David's son Solomon fulfilled the covenant. But they'd only be partly right. Only Jesus can ultimately fulfill it.

As you read through 1 Chronicles (or any other book for that matter), don't underestimate the order in which a biblical writer presents his material. The fact that the tribe of Judah is listed first in the national genealogy (2:3–15) is not coincidental. The writer is quietly celebrating that the monarchy, the temple construction, and the future Messiah (Jesus) will come from this tribe.

And one more thing. Unlike our Bible, the Hebrew Bible ends with the Book of Chronicles. Think of it. This lineage of Israel headlined by the tribe of Judah (ch. 1—9) is a preamble to the genealogy of Jesus in the first chapter of the first book of the New Testament.

2 Chronicles

By the time we get into the second volume of the chronicles of Israel's kings, we discover that it parallels the two Books of Kings. There is one major exception, however.

The writer of 2 Chronicles virtually ignores the northern kingdom of Israel because of its false worship and refusal to acknowledge the temple in Jerusalem. Instead this writer focuses on those who pattern their lives and reigns after a more godly King David who is a prototype of the coming Messiah.

Even after the southern kingdom has fallen and the throne of David has been destroyed, the line of David from which Jesus will be born remains. It's amazing. This book reads like a novel. There's war, murder, and treachery, as attempts are made to chop down the messianic family tree. But the tree survives and the fulfillment can be seen in the unbroken genealogies of Matthew 1 and Luke 3.

The temple in 2 Chronicles is spotlighted in chapters 2 and 7. It suggests the Incarnation of Jesus. Just try this verse on for size. "But will God indeed dwell with men on earth?" (6:18). This verse does more than announce God's coming presence. It anticipates the way Jesus will deal with the need of sinful people to be forgiven by virtue of a perfect sacrifice. As beautiful and complex as the temple was, Jesus would later say of Himself, "In this place there is one greater than the temple" (Matthew 12:6). But that's not all. Jesus also likens His body to the temple (John 2:19). In fact, according to the Book of Revelation, at the end of time Jesus, the Lamb of God, will replace the need for an earthly temple (Revelation 22:21).

This book reads like a novel. There's war, murder, and treachery, as attempts are made to chop down the messianic family tree.

Ezra

By the end of the Chronicles we must begin to wonder what happens next. Fortunately, the account of Ezra, the priest, describes how the exiled Jews make

their way back to Jerusalem in two separate installments. Do we see explicit reference to Jesus in his
book? Well, not exactly. But the inferences are unmistakable.

Ezra reveals God's continued fulfillment of His promise to keep David's descendents alive. Zerubbabel,
the grandson of Jeconiah, is not just
another man with an odd-sounding
name. He is part of Jesus' earthly
genealogy (1 Chronicles 3:17–19;
Matthew 1:12–13). It may seem insignificant that the remnant of David's extended family had to return
to Jerusalem. But it isn't. The posi-
tive turn of events sets up the good
fortune that will give way to the
Good News of Jesus. Without access
to the original "land of promise,"
Jesus couldn't have been born in

As Ezra documents the return from Babylon, the soundtrack of forgiveness and restoration plays in the background. It is a melody line that will accompany the life, death, and Resurrection of Jesus.

Bethlehem, which was a requirement for the Messiah
(Micah 5:2). As Ezra documents the return from
Babylon, the soundtrack of forgiveness and restoration plays in the background. It is a melody line that
will accompany the life, death, and Resurrection of

Jesus. It is music to God's ears to hear His people confess and repent (1:1).

Nehemiah

But not everyone returned to Jerusalem with Ezra. The third and final resettlement of Jews from Babylon to Israel was recorded by a man named Nehemiah. His concern for the welfare of Jerusalem and its inhabitants is not unlike that of the One who willingly came from the King's presence in heaven to earth (Matthew 23:37). Like Jesus, Nehemiah gives up a high position in order to identify with the plight of his people. Like Jesus he comes with a specific mission and accomplishes it. And get this. Just like Jesus, Nehemiah's life is punctuated by his prayerful dependence on God (1:5; Luke 6:12). His purpose is not just to get the Jews back to Jerusalem. No, his ultimate goal is restoration! The temple is rebuilt. The city walls are repaired. Jerusalem is reconstructed. The covenant is renewed, and the people are reformed. Talk about an indirect reference to Jesus. It doesn't get much more obvious. According to the apostle Paul, reconciliation and renewal was why Jesus came into our world (2 Corinthians 5:18).

Like a jigsaw puzzle coming together, Nehemiah's

pieces provide a picture of what's to come. But a major piece is missing. Although much is restored and the messianic line is intact, the king has not yet arrived. But not to worry. The decree that Artaxerxes, the king of Babylon, makes in the twentieth year of his reign (2:2) marks the beginning point of the prophetic "seventy weeks" that the prophet Daniel talks about in the book named for him. The seventy weeks provide a timetable for the Messiah's arrival. "Know therefore and understand that from the going forth of the command to restore and build Jerusalem until Messiah the Prince, there shall be seven weeks and sixty-two weeks . . ." (Daniel 9:25–27). And guess what? This prophecy about the Anointed One of God arriving at the end of sixty-nine weeks culminated in A.D. 33. That is the year many think that Jesus appeared on the scene.

Esther

An inspiring story about a brave and godly young woman is set in the same time period as the Books of Ezra and Nehemiah. The Book of Esther is written to the Jews who didn't return to Jerusalem (for whatever reason). It's intended to encourage them to trust God and be faithful. In it we see a dramatic portrayal of redemption that whets our appetite for what only Christ can do.

Esther puts herself in harm's way for her people as she attempts to be an advocate. The similarities to Jesus' mission on our behalf are staggering. Whereas Esther's rise to power was orchestrated by God "for such a time as this" (4:14), the apostle Paul describes Jesus' entrance into our world as something that occurred "when the fullness of the time had come" (Galatians 4:4).

Another remarkable similarity between Esther's story and Jesus is the Satanic attempt to destroy the divine plot of redemption God set in motion. But, in both cases God brings about His purpose by preserving His people in spite of opposition and danger. Thanks to the Book of Esther, we not only see a foreshadowing of Jesus' sacrifice on our behalf, but we also see how God maintained the family tree on which would blossom the "rose of Sharon."

CHAPTER THREE

Jesus in the Poetical Books

Job

As we saw in the books of Moses, the promise of a Savior was quite pronounced from the beginning of time to the time of the Exodus. In the uneven development of Israel (as chronicled by the authors of the historical books), God continues to give hints that He had a plan that would culminate in a person known as the Messiah. Within the Old Testament, an entirely different genre of literature is grouped together to illustrate God's truth through human experiences of daily routines, worship, heartaches, and love. We call these books "poetical." These songs, poems, and journal entries also include the lyrics of love that would be sung by God's Son one day.

The first book in this category is thought by many scholars to be the oldest book in the Bible. Job's story gives us a glimpse into the heart of a man who loses everything and wrestles with God in an attempt to understand why. Job suffers greatly, yet in the grip of unimaginable hardship, he acknowledges his Redeemer is still in control (19:25–27). Feeling maligned and misunderstood, he cries out for a mediator (9:33; 25:4; 33:23).

Although Jesus is not named in the Book of Job, He is the only one Job could have been referring to. No one else can be called our Redeemer. No other book in the Bible includes such graphic detail of the problems and questions that skeptics and believers alike wrestle with or ask. If you haven't read Job recently, do it. You will see the wide range of human hurts that Jesus identified with in His earthly life as well as the ones He empathizes with as He intercedes for us in heaven (Hebrews 4:15).

It is not insignificant that in the very first chapter of Job we are introduced to an earthly man who, though not perfect, is extraordinarily upright and godly. As a Christ-figure, Job is denied any hedge of protection and thus is exposed to the raw reality of a sinful world. Isn't that exactly what happened to Jesus?

Psalms

Finding Jesus in the Book of Job is a bit more of a challenge than finding references to Him in the Psalms. The Psalms are full of allusions to Him! The

"One to come" is a frequently repeated theme of these ancient Hebrew worship songs. Many specifically anticipate the life and ministry of Jesus Christ, the One who came centuries later as the promised Messiah. But unless you know what you're looking for, you just might miss these special references.

It helps if you think in terms of five different categories of psalms that point to Jesus. The first kind is the typical messianic kind. That simply means that the subject of the particular psalm is in some way a type of what Jesus will one day be. For example, Psalm 69:4 has the psalmist acknowledging "those who hate me without a cause are more than the hairs of my head." (See also 34:20; 69:9.)

If you look closely you can detect that the writer is describing more than just what he is experiencing.

A second kind of messianic psalm is the typical prophetic. In these, the psalmist uses language to describe present circumstances in which there is more there than meets the eye. If you look closely you can detect that the writer is describing more than just what he is experiencing. He is pointing beyond his experience to something that will be historically true of Jesus, too (ch. 22).

A third category is the indirectly messianic. In this category of psalm, reference is made to the current king or the house of David in general. But guess what? The primary meaning can only be understood in the future when the Anointed One makes His promised appearance. (See Psalm 2, 45, and 72.)

The purely prophetic is the fourth kind of messianic psalm. As this category suggests, these psalms can only be understood in reference to Jesus. No king of Israel or descendent of David is fulfilling them. An example of this is Psalm 110:1, "The Lord said to my Lord, 'Sit at My right hand, Till I make Your enemies Your footstool.'"

But there is one more kind of messianic psalm that points to Jesus. It is called the enthronement psalm. Anticipating the day when Yahweh (Jehovah) will consummate His kingdom in the person of the Messiah, the psalmists write with both eyes focused on eternity. There's no way this kind of psalm makes sense in the present (meaning the time when it was written). (See Psalm 96—99.)

Proverbs

In Psalms, while hearing the songs of a nation at worship, we are invited to look through a telescope

aimed far into the future. In Proverbs, we find ourselves looking at life through a microscope of scrutiny.
These short capsules of insight magnify the importance of wise choices and the tragic consequences
that occur when we make foolish ones. They are mostly
written by David's son, Solomon.

Although Jesus is not identified by name in chapter eight, it is clear that the writer is describing Him.
(See Proverbs 8:22–31.) Wisdom, godlike and perfect, is personified. "I have been established from
everlasting, from the beginning, before there was ever
an earth." (Compare Proverbs 8:23 with John 1:1.)
But there's more. This divine wisdom is also the
source of biological and spiritual life (3:18; 8:35). It
is right and moral (8:8–9), and it is available to all
who will receive it.

When you stop and think about it, that is almost
exactly the way the apostle John describes the divine
Word's entrance into the world. "But as many as
received Him, to them He gave the right to become
children of God, to those who believe on His name"
(John 1:12).

The wisdom that King Solomon says is available
to whoever is willing to receive it is the same wisdom
the apostle Paul claims became incarnate in Christ,

"In whom are hidden all the treasures of wisdom and knowledge" (Colossians 2:3). Or as Paul writes to the Corinthians, "But of Him you are in Christ Jesus who became for us wisdom from God" (1 Corinthians 1:22–24, 30).

As we peer into the looking glass and see the sad state of life lived apart from the Lord, we recognize that only in Jesus can ultimate satisfaction, wisdom, and joy be found.

Ecclesiastes

If Psalms is a telescope and Proverbs is a microscope, Ecclesiastes is a mirror. In it we see a less-than-flattering reflection of who we are and how we feel much of the time. Here's a book also penned by King Solomon but during a more jaded time in his life. It's a candid commentary on the emptiness and inner perplexity that marks the life of one who is disconnected from his Creator. It's a journal of honest doubts, hopes, and fears.

Because each person on earth has "eternity in his heart" (3:11), there is a purpose for Jesus to divest Himself of His divine dignity and descend to our sinful planet. In that we bear God's image, He desires to enter our world to provide the necessary remedy in order to maximize our eternal potential. As we peer into the looking glass and see the sad state of life lived apart from the Lord, we recognize that only in Jesus can ultimate satisfaction, wisdom, and joy be found.

Solomon makes specific reference to "one Shepherd" who offers abundant life (12:11; see also John 10:9–10). As with other biblical writers, Solomon's use of the singular "one" leaves little doubt as to whom he means.

Song of Solomon

Solomon is quite prolific with his pen. His propensity to publish must be connected to the wealth of wisdom he possesses. He thinks deeply and shares his insights liberally. Fortunately for us, he writes lyrics of a love song that celebrated his romantic passions while at the same time picturing a perfect love he knows he is not capable of.

Throughout the Old Testament, the nation of Israel is regarded as the bride of Yahweh. Passages like Isaiah 54:5 illustrate the relationship. "For your Maker is your husband, the Lord of hosts is His name." But this is just one of many. (See also Jeremiah 2:2; Ezekiel 16:8–14; Hosea 2:16–20.)

Just as some of the psalms have a contemporary application as well as a future-oriented one, so the

entire Song of Solomon has three levels of fulfillment. The encounters and affectionate exchanges
between Solomon and his bride are passionate poetry
documenting human love. But the king also illustrates God's love for the people of God over whom
he rules. And Solomon's ornamental language also
prefigures the delight and joy Jesus has for His Bride
and His unconditional commitment to His Church.
In the New Testament the followers of Jesus are seen
as the personified object of His love. (See 2 Corinthians 11:2; Ephesians 5:23–25; Revelation 19:7–9;
21:9.)

CHAPTER FOUR

Jesus in the Major Prophets

Isaiah

The references to the Messiah in poetry, praise, pithy wisdom, and love lyrics are filled with imagery and wonder. But the poetical books in the Hebrew Bible do not tell the whole story. They do not convey the breadth of judgment and hope associated with the Messiah's coming. Another grouping of books does that. This section is typically referred to as the major prophets, and for good reason. Besides the fact that their message is of big-league proportion, Isaiah, Jeremiah, Ezekiel, and Daniel also use a major amount of ink and parchment.

That's certainly true of Isaiah. It consists of sixty-six chapters written over forty years of his ministry. Isaiah's prophecies span the reign of four kings in Judah. And when he makes reference to the coming Messiah, this prophet sounds more like a New Testament writer than an Old Testament one. In other words, his references to Jesus are clear and explicit.

While other messianic allusions in the Old Testament are abstract or cumbersome, Isaiah sees with unprecedented clarity.

For example, he writes, "Therefore the Lord Himself will give you a sign: Behold the virgin shall conceive

In all, there are more than three hundred prophecies in the Old Testament concerning the first advent of Jesus.

and bear a son and shall call His name Immanuel" (7:14). That is entirely fulfilled by the events leading up to Jesus' birth. Go ahead. Check it out by reading Matthew 1:22–23.

And there is much more. Isaiah refers to Jesus' earthly ministry and His Crucifixion as well as His eventual return to earth as a reigning King. Often, however, those references are woven together and need to be viewed through the context of history.

Here are a few more of Isaiah's Christological prophecies and their New Testament fulfillments: Isaiah 9:6 gives way to Luke 2:11 and Ephesians 2:14–18. Isaiah 50:6 plays out with unbelievable precision in Matthew 26:67; 27:26, 30. And Isaiah 61:1–2 is nothing less than the personal mission Jesus verbalizes and embraces when He reads the scroll at the synagogue in Nazareth. That's recorded in Luke 4:17–19.

In all, there are more than three hundred prophecies in the Old Testament concerning the first advent of Jesus. Isaiah contributes many of these. But he also has incorporated an amazing number of references to Jesus' Second Coming. They include Isaiah 4:2; 11:2–6, 10; 32:1–8; 49:7; 52:13, 15; 59:20–21; 60:1–3; 61:2–3.

Of particular importance is Isaiah's description of the five aspects of Jesus' saving work on our behalf. They appear in the five stanzas of Isaiah 52:13—53:12. There we read of Jesus' wholehearted sacrifice, His perfect character, His atonement that results in peace with God, His payment that results in our forgiveness, and His death that nullifies the effects of sin.

Jeremiah

Like Isaiah, Jeremiah spoke on behalf of God for more than forty years. In much the same way, he also couched his warnings of God's judgment to the kings and people of Judah with compassion. Although Jeremiah's references to Jesus are not as numerous as Isaiah's, they are equally as strong. He paints a word picture of the Messiah in 23:1–8 in which we see Him as the coming Shepherd and righteous Branch who "shall reign and prosper and execute judgment and righteousness to the earth . . . now this is His name by which He will be called: The Lord our Righteousness" (Isaiah 23:5–6).

But Jeremiah doesn't stop there. He writes of one who "will bring in the new covenant" (31:31–34). This is the same one who will fulfill God's covenants with Abraham (Genesis 12:1–3; 17:1–8), the ones between Moses and the people (Deuteronomy 28—30), and the one with David (2 Samuel 7:1–17).

Jeremiah makes reference to a curse that is placed on King Jehoiachin (Coniah) in 22:24–30. The bottom line of this judgment from God is that none of this wayward king's descendants will rule Israel. Curiously, in Matthew's genealogy in which he traces Jesus' earthly lineage (Matthew 1:1–17), Joseph is a descendent of this cursed king. You'd think this would be a problem since no son of Joseph could ascend to Israel's throne. But, since Jesus' true earthly line flows through His mother, Luke traces Christ's lineage backwards from Mary through a son of David who is not related to Jehoiachin (Luke 3:23–38). By doing this, Jesus escapes the curse. It makes a way for Jeremiah's righteous Branch to reign on David's throne.

Lamentations

Even Jeremiah is not content to communicate God's message to Israel in straight narrative. He borrows Solomon's pen to write a five-poem dirge to express his emotions. The prophet grieves over the destruction of a disobedient city. Jerusalem lies barren as a result of the invading Babylonian armies.

This weeping prophet is a type of Jesus. Six centuries later, it is the Son of God who weeps over the same city.

In his mournful lyrics Jeremiah does more than focus on his feelings. His vulnerable grief focuses our attention on the One who is to come. This weeping prophet is a type of Jesus. Six centuries later, it is the Son of God who weeps over the same city. "O Jerusalem, Jerusalem. The one who kills the prophets and stones those who are sent to her. How often I wanted to gather your children together as a hen gathers her chicks under her wings, but you were not willing! See! Your house is left to you desolate!" (Matthew 23:37–38).

It's amazing. Just like Jesus, Jeremiah identifies himself personally with the plight of Jerusalem and with the human suffering caused by sin. "My eyes flow and do not cease without interruption till the Lord from heaven looks down and sees. My eyes bring suffering to my soul because of all the daughters of my city" (3:49–50).

This tear-stained prophet also provides an accurate description of the one Isaiah called "a Man of sorrows and acquainted with grief" (Isaiah 53:3). Jeremiah speaks of the Messiah's being afflicted (1:12; 3:19), despised, and derided by His enemies (2:15–16; 3:14, 30).

Ezekiel

Isaiah and Jeremiah were not the only ones speaking for God when the Babylonians threatened to and then silenced the voices of His people. In Judah's darkest hour, Ezekiel dramatized God's messages to those exiled far from Jerusalem. And like the others, this prophet described the Holy One of God who would step onto the stage of history after the curtain fell on the Old Testament and a several-hundred-year intermission finished.

Because he was a hostage in Babylon with those to whom he prophesied, Ezekiel knew what it was like to lack strength. Wouldn't you think that would account for the way he described the Messiah as being "a tender twig that becomes a stately cedar on a lofty mountain?" (17:22–24) That's an image not unlike the Branch that Isaiah writes about in the first verse of his eleventh chapter. Jeremiah also talks about the

Branch. (See Jeremiah 23:5; 33:15.) As a matter of fact, even Zechariah, one of the minor prophets, refers to the Branch (Zechariah 3:8—6:12).

For Ezekiel, the One who is coming to be Israel's ultimate King will have the lone right to rule over the people God has chosen to be His. A unique people can only be led by a unique individual. And until He appears, the prophet demands that those who would attempt to mount the throne prematurely "remove the turban and take off the crown" (21:26).

Ezekiel is confident that day will come. His confidence is reflected in the additional metaphor that he uses to call attention to that hope. Describing a field far from the palace, he pictures God's Anointed as the true Shepherd who will deliver and feed His flock (34:11–31).

Daniel

Ezekiel had company in the far country. His countryman was a Jewish hostage who had 20/20 vision when it came to looking into the future. Long before Daniel was locked in a lion's cave, he was a teenager locked out of his home in Jerusalem and taken captive to Babylon. But from the palace in which Daniel was privileged to live, God gave him a room with a view. He was able to see what would happen to the people of God long after they had returned from captivity. He saw the fulfillment of Israel's life-long hope.

In the book that bears his name, Daniel pictures Jesus as the great Stone who will crush the kingdoms of this world (2:34–35, 44). With his love of imagery, the prophet also describes the Messiah as the Son of Man who is given dominion by the Ancient of Days (7:13–14). Jesus is also portrayed as Israel's Deliverer who will be cut off (9:25–26).

> *Daniel's precise prediction is unlike any other biblical writer's. He pinpoints the birth of Jesus five hundred years beforehand.*

Daniel's dreams and visions fill his book. It is possible that his vision in 10:5–9 is an appearance of Christ Himself (similar to what the apostle John describes in Revelation 1:12–16). Daniel's precise prediction is unlike any other biblical writer's. He pinpoints the birth of Jesus five hundred years beforehand. It's the amazing vision of the sixty-nine weeks (9:25–26). Based on what Nehemiah tells us (Nehemiah 2:1–8), the decree about which Daniel writes in verse 25 took place on March 4, 444 B.C.

When each week is considered equivalent to seven years, the 69 weeks equate to 483 years. Using a 360-day calendar, you could also calculate that to be 173,880 days. Beginning with March 4, 444 B.C., the 173,880-day period takes us to March 29, A.D. 33. No, that wasn't the birth of Jesus, but it is thought to be the date when He made His triumphal entry into Jerusalem. Go ahead and check it out if you want. From 444 B.C. to A.D. 33 is 476 years. And 476 years times 365.24219 days per year equals 173,855 days. When you add to that number 25 more days for the difference between March 4 and March 29, you arrive at—you guessed it—173,880 days. The prophecies are startling in their absolute precision.

CHAPTER FIVE

Jesus in the Minor Prophets

Hosea

Those who wrote the Old Testament were a rag tag collection of humanity. God inspired each with the means and the message and the opportunity. Some wrote large tomes. Others were less prolific. Those commonly termed "minor prophets" were distinguished by the fact that their books were shorter. Please don't give in to the false notion that their message was any less important than the major prophets'. Nothing could be further from the truth.

Consider Hosea for instance. His penetrating message directed at the northern kingdom (Israel) exposes both their unfaithful tendencies and God's undeserved love. Although the nation is experiencing a time of prosperity and growth, it is decaying inwardly due to corruption and spiritual adultery.

If you know Hosea's story, you know that the Lord asks this godly man to marry a prostitute named Gomer and remain faithful. His commitment in the marriage in which his wife is anything but faithful is a picture of God's determination to stand by Israel in spite of their rejection and His heartache.

After reading Hosea, it's only natural to think of Jesus, the sinless Son of God, coming to a sin-prone planet. He demonstrates His love and commitment and yet is rejected and betrayed. But there's more than an implied metaphor here. Matthew applies Hosea 11:1 to the infant Jesus exiled in Egypt with His parents. "When Israel was a child I loved him and out of Egypt I called my son" (Matthew 2:6). What Matthew is doing is quoting the second half of this verse to show that the Exodus of Israel from Egypt as a new nation was a forecast of Israel's Messiah, who was also called out of Egypt in His childhood. Both Israel and Jesus left the land to take refuge for a time in Pharaoh's country.

But the most compelling portrait of Jesus in Hosea is how Hosea redeems Gomer from the slave market. When reading this, you can't help but see Jesus' identifying with our plight and lovingly paying the cost of our freedom with His blood.

Joel

It's mind-boggling how God uses the most unexpected circumstances to get the attention of His peo-

ple. And His prophets. With Hosea, it was the call
to marry a woman of ill-repute. For Joel, it was the
challenge of making sense out of a locust plague.
Without forewarning Judah was laid bare—literally.
And Joel, inspired by the Holy Spirit, explained how
tragedy is sometimes God's instrument to get our attention.

Joel spoke on behalf of a holy God to explain the
Almighty's actions toward a people He claims as His
own. That's exactly what Jesus, God's premier Spokes-
person, did. But there is a more direct correlation to
Jesus in Joel than that. Remember when Jesus promised the disciples that He would send the Holy Spirit
after His Ascension into heaven? (See John 16:7–15;
Acts 1:8.) Well, when this was fulfilled on the Day
of Pentecost, Peter said, "This is what was spoken by
the prophet Joel, 'And it shall come to pass in the last
days,' says God, 'that I will pour out My spirit on all
flesh . . .'" (Acts 2:16–17). And Peter is attribut-
ing the fulfillment of Jesus' promise directly to Joel
2:28–32.

In Joel 3:2,12 the prophet anticipates a gathering
of all nations in the valley of Jehoshaphat, where
the Anointed One of God (Jesus) will judge among
them.

Amos

Whereas Joel prophesied during Judah's perilous plague of locusts, Amos took to the pulpit during a period of national optimism in Israel. Business was booming, and boundaries were bulging. But don't be fooled. God fingered this fruit picker to wave a clenched fist at a greedy and unjust people. It's quite possible Jesus was thinking of Amos when He pointed His finger at the Pharisees and mocked their surface-deep appearances.

God fingered this fruit picker to wave a clenched fist at a greedy and unjust people.

Amos came from an insignificant village by the name of Tekoa. He was a sheep breeder and a tender of sycamore fruit, yet God used this blue-collar worker as the means by which His people might see the red face of His anger. Can you see it? Amos is a type of Jesus who also came from a tiny town on the other side of the tracks and who, though a common laborer, provided us with the face of God's wrath as well as His love.

Though most of Amos's prophecy is about God's authority to judge an apathetic ungrateful nation, he ends his books with the promise that God will restore

His people and raise up the "Tabernacle of David" (9:11). This obviously refers to more than just the kingdom of David and the temple his son Solomon built. It speaks of the fulfillment of the Davidic dynasty, which finds its focus in the Son of David—Jesus.

Obadiah

Have you ever wondered how a single-chapter book bearing the odd name of the prophet who wrote it could end up in the Old Testament? Obadiah's name means "servant of God," and like Jesus, the supreme Servant of God (whom Isaiah spoke about), this prophet has his work cut out for him. Like Jesus, he has the difficult task of representing Yahweh to those who don't want to hear what he has to say.

Obadiah's audience was the Edomites, Esau's descendants. Time and again they had snubbed God's people—the descendents of Jacob, Esau's twin brother. Because of their calloused hatred, God channeled His judgment toward them. Obadiah is the Lord's mouthpiece as he stands up for Israel and sounds off against Edom. In his prophecy this little known prophet anticipates the One who will come to judge the nations (vv. 15–16). He also makes reference to the Savior of Israel. "But on Mount Zion there shall be deliverance and there shall be holiness . . ." (vv. 17–20).

Jonah

Working your way through the minor prophets, it's easy to feel swallowed up by all the unfamiliar details so different from our culture. But in Jonah we see a man who, though swallowed by a huge fish, struggles to obey the call of God just like we do.

In spite of his initial reluctance to accept God's appointment to Nineveh, once Jonah gets there and starts to preach, we see a preview of coming attractions. He proclaims, like Jesus later will, the need to repent. And the book that claims his name also illustrates that God is a merciful God who withholds His punishment to people who respond to Him. Jesus taught the same.

Could that be why Jonah is the only prophet Jesus identified as a symbol of Himself? Listen to what Jesus said: "An evil and adulterous generation seeks after a sign and no sign will be given to it except the sign of the prophet Jonah . . ." (Matthew 12:39). And then we see how much Jonah's story is a type of Jesus' life, death, and Resurrection. "For as Jonah was three days and three nights in the belly of the great fish, so will the Son of Man be three days and three nights in the heart of the earth . . . and indeed greater than Jonah is here" (Matthew 12:30–41).

Micah

Micah was more willing to do God's bidding than Jonah, even though it meant leaving his familiar rural roots to parade in front of kings in the palace in Jerusalem. Unlike the Book of Jonah, which took the burial and Resurrection of Jesus for Israel to make sense out of what had occurred, Micah's reference to the Messiah was quite explicit. From the time he verbalized God's rebuke at the way the Jews were treating the poor until the time a poor carpenter and his young wife arrived in Bethlehem, devout Jews knew that King David's birthplace was where the Messiah would also be born.

Could that be why Jonah is the only prophet Jesus identified as a symbol of Himself?

Micah wrote the following seven hundred years before Jesus was born: "Though you are little among the thousands of Judah, yet out of you shall come forth to Me the One to be Ruler in Israel, whose goings forth are from of old, from everlasting" (5:2).

When questioned by Herod about where the king of

the Jews was to be born, the chief priests and scribes referred to Micah's words. In addition, this little book of prophecy also provides us one of the best descriptions in the entire Bible about the righteous reign of Christ (when He comes again). "He will teach us His ways and we shall walk in His paths . . . nation shall not lift up sword against nation, neither shall they learn war anymore" (4:2–4).

Nahum

These minor prophets offer a smorgasbord of messages about and inferences to the coming Messiah. Whereas Micah's prediction of Jesus' birthplace is irrefutable, Nahum does not specifically mention the Messiah or David's throne. But it would be shortsighted to imply from this absence of specifics that he doesn't have a vision for the coming One.

Nahum himself is a type of Christ. His name means comfort, yet this one called a comforter does not offer soft love. Nahum, like Jesus, expects responsible action on the part of those who are loved by God. Such action is a way to prove that they acknowledge His love.

Nahum's ministry in Nineveh comes one hundred years after they responded to Jonah's preaching.

Because his name means comforter, it is legitimate to say he pictures the Holy Spirit's subsequent ministry of instruction and comfort that Jesus promised His followers. "He will teach you all things and bring to your remembrance all things that I said to you" (John 14:26). But sadly, similar to the rejection Jesus faced at the hand of the scribes and Pharisees, the Ninevites do not act on what Nahum teaches them.

As this minor prophet begins his prophecy, he waxes eloquently about the divine attributes of the One who will judge the nations at the end of time. They are words that obviously refer to the One who claims to know His sheep by name (John 10:3). "The Lord is good, a stronghold in the day of trouble. And He knows those who trust in Him . . ." (1:7).

Habakkuk

As we continue to look for references throughout the Bible for the One who became flesh and dwelt among us in order to embrace us with God's unmerited mercy (John 1:14), we come to the Book of Habakkuk. It's an odd sounding name to us, and it was an unusual name in his time as well. It is derived from the Hebrew word for "embrace." As Habakkuk concludes his ministry to an unrepentant Southern

Kingdom, he continues to cling to the God who called him to share his unpopular message of judgment (3:16–19).

But Habakkuk's name is also appropriate because he calls attention to the salvation by which God embraces those who "live by faith." The word "salvation" appears three times in reference to his prediction of the Anointed One. "You went forth for the salvation of Your people with Your Anointed. . . . I will joy in the God of my salvation" (3:13, 18).

Interestingly enough, that Hebrew word for "salvation" is the root word from which the name "Jesus" comes.

Interestingly enough, that Hebrew word for "salvation" is the root word from which the name "Jesus" comes (Matthew 1:21). Whether the prophet sees the full extent to which Jesus will accomplish the world's salvation is uncertain. But he definitely sees an artist's rendering of the reign of Christ. He writes, "The earth will be filled with the knowledge of the glory of the Lord as the waters cover the sea" (2:14).

Zephaniah

But lest you stare at Habakkuk's portrait of Israel's preferred future too long, step up to the next canvas in the minor prophets' gallery. Zephaniah's forceful prophecy is delivered during Judah's hectic political and religious history. His announcement of a coming day of the Lord results in widespread repentance and reform. How the other minor prophets would have loved that!

Jesus seized on Zephaniah's picture of the day of the Lord. On one occasion He referred to Zephaniah 1:3, when He spoke of His Second Coming and gathering "out of His kingdom all things that offend and those who practice lawlessness" (Matthew 13:41). On another occasion, Jesus no doubt envisioned Zephaniah's description of "that day of wrath, a day of trouble and distress, a day of devastation and desolation, a day of darkness and gloominess, a day of clouds and thick darkness, a day of trumpet and alarm" (1:15–16).

On that particular occasion the Savior anticipated His eventual return to reign on earth and said, "The sun will be darkened and the moon will not give its light . . . and all the tribes on earth will mourn and they will see the Son of Man coming on the clouds . . . and He will send His angels with a great sound of a trumpet . . ." (Matthew 24:29–31).

Although Zephaniah doesn't specifically name the Messiah as the subject of these scenarios, it is assumed. Who else could, as the prophet foretells, gather His people and reign in victory?

Haggai

Throughout the history of Israel we observe a two-step dance of staggered devotion. One foot steps toward God but soon the other one steps away. When Haggai arrives on the scene, the people of God have returned from Babylon to Jerusalem. But after sixteen years they have not rebuilt the temple—the tangible indicator of God's abiding presence. Their behavior, resembling a dance of indecision, means they have not jumped in with both feet to celebrate their return from exile.

Whenever Jesus set foot inside, the presence of the incarnate God filled this temple with the glory of which Haggai spoke.

When Haggai writes "The glory of this latter temple shall be greater than the former" (2:9), he is certainly referring to the reconstructed temple Herod would enlarge. Whenever Jesus set foot inside, the presence of the incarnate God filled this temple with the glory of which Haggai spoke.

Beyond this prophet's words, we also see the Messiah represented in one of Haggai's peers whom we meet in the book. Zerubbabel is the governor of Judah after the exiles return. Based on what the Lord has told him to say, Haggai declares that Zerubbabel will become the signet ring of the Most High. In other words, he will be the proof of God's authority. Although Jesus will be the eventual Signet, Zerubbabel becomes the center of the messianic line for a time. Like a king's ring he seals both the pre-exilic and post-exilic branch of David's lineage together.

Zechariah

As we near the end of the minor prophets, we are introduced to Zechariah. He spoke on God's behalf during the same time period as Haggai. God gave him a similar message to share with the people. "Finish the temple!" After returning from exile and beginning reconstruction of the temple, the Jews stalled in their efforts. For a dozen years or more, the temple sat half-completed.

But rather than exhorting the people with strong words of rebuke, Zechariah motivates the people by casting a vision. Like Jesus, Zechariah looks forward to the coming kingdom. He reminds God's people of the future importance of the temple. It is to be a holy building that houses the glory of the Messiah.

Like Micah, Zechariah includes clear passages that point to God's Anointed One. Jesus is portrayed in His First and Second Comings as both servant/king and man/God respectively. Why not discover the way the prophet pictures Jesus firsthand? He appears as the angel of the Lord (3:1–2), the Righteous Branch (3:8; 6:12–13), and the King-Priest (6:13).

You may struggle to see how Zechariah depicts the Messiah as the cornerstone, tent peg, and battle bow in chapter ten, verse four, but the effort is worth it.

His description of Jesus as the good Shepherd who is rejected and sold for thirty shekels of silver is a precise prediction.

A much more obvious reference to Jesus is found in Zechariah 9:9–10, where the prophet anticipates the Savior's triumphal entry into Jerusalem on that first Palm Sunday. His description of Jesus as the good Shepherd who is rejected and sold for thirty shekels of silver is a precise prediction (11:11–13).

The same is true of 12:10, in which the Messiah is pierced and in 13:7, in which the smitten Shepherd is abandoned. And in chapter 14 of Zechariah, we see Jesus as the coming Judge and righteous King.

Malachi

You'd think that with all the prophetic voices the Jews were forced to listen to, they would have toed the mark. But the fact that God needed Malachi indicates otherwise. He was a contemporary of Nehemiah. Rather than getting down on the people, Malachi directed his message to Israel's spiritual leaders. The priests had become lax and corrupt. They allowed mixed marriages, idolatry, and divorce.

Malachi's name means "messenger." His life's calling from God was to clarify the message the priests had bumbled. But in his prophecy he also predicts the coming of another messenger whose ministry will precede the Messiah and clear the way for His coming. "Behold, I send My messenger. And he will prepare the way before Me . . ." (3:1). In his mind this messenger would be someone like Elijah—one who would call parents to repent and turn the hearts of the children to their fathers (4:5–6). From our perspective we know that he was referring to Jesus' cousin John (who resembled Elijah in more ways than one).

Still Malachi is not only referring to the first appearance of Jesus. He also gives us a glimpse of Jesus' encore performance as the returning and reigning king.

"But who can endure the day of His coming? And who can stand when He appears? For He is like a refiner's fire and like launderer's soap" (3:2). If you think those words remind you of music you hear at Christmas, you're right. George F. Handel borrowed generously from Malachi in choosing biblical passages for his oratorio *Messiah*. And why not? Where else but in Malachi do we see specific references to Jesus as the Sun of Righteousness rising "with healing in His wings" (4:2)?

Jesus
In the
New Testament

CHAPTER SIX

Jesus in the Gospels

Matthew

As we move from the Old Testament into the New Testament, we leave behind the parchments on which the prophets probed the future in search of indicators of the promised Messiah. Now we look at the life and teachings of Jesus, who has come.

Perhaps you've heard the old saying that compares the two Testaments that comprise our Bible. "Jesus is in the Old Testament concealed, but He is in the New Testament revealed." That says it simply yet accurately. But we must be cautious not to let our familiarity with this second half of the Scriptures blind us to nuances we might otherwise miss.

In the first four books of the New Testament we find similar material. It should not surprise anybody that Jesus is front and center in the four Gospels. That's

> *"Jesus is in the Old Testament concealed, but He is in the New Testament revealed."*

why they were written. Jesus' life is tracked with near chronological exactness in Matthew, Mark, and Luke. But each author underscores or overlooks certain elements in order to accomplish a particular purpose dictated by the needs of his unique readership.

Matthew, as a Jew, unashamedly shapes his account about Jesus' life so it is understood by a Jewish audience. His goal is to convince his peers that the King of kings has come. With this in mind, he uses terms and names that Jews will resonate with. By quoting more passages from the Old Testament than any other New Testament writer, he attempts to validate that Jesus is indeed the promised Messiah. No less than twelve times Matthew presents Jesus as Israel's messianic king (1:23; 2:2, 6; 3:17; 4:15–17; 21:5, 9; 22:44–45; 26:64; 27:11, 27–37).

Also unique to Matthew is the expression, "that it might be fulfilled which was spoken by the prophet." By footnoting familiar passages the Jews accepted as God's inspired Word, Matthew builds his case for Christ with the precision of a former tax collector. Examine for yourself how he substantiates the prophecies that pointed to Jesus' miraculous and obscure birth, His birthplace, His exile to Egypt and return to Israel, and His rejection and suffering. No wonder Matthew begins his book with an impressive genealogy of Jesus' link to King David.

Mark

Whereas Matthew was written by a tax collector who became one of Jesus' twelve disciples, Mark was written by a young disciple of Peter. In fact, most believe Mark put into writing what he'd heard Peter preach over many years. As a careful reading will bear out, it is likely that both Matthew and Luke use Mark's content as the outline for their individual biographies of Jesus.

Mark leaves no doubt that he is documenting a unique account of a unique man. He's spotlighting the Son of Man who came from heaven to serve, not to be served, and to give His life as a ransom (10:45). So in Mark we see Jesus the obedient Servant of God actively and compassionately coming alongside hurting people. But it's not just the physical hurts that haunt Him. Jesus is moved by the spiritual disease He sees all around Him.

If Mark's intent is to present Jesus as a humble Servant, there is no need for an impressive family tree (like Matthew and Luke include). That is why the author begins with Jesus' public ministry and with

Mark's frequent use of the word "immediately" (used more in this compact book than all the rest of the New Testament). Jesus is continually on the move. Even though He knows He has a limited time to fulfill the purpose for which He came to earth, others don't. What they do come to understand is that Jesus viewed

If Mark's intent is to present Jesus as a humble servant, there is no need for an impressive family tree (like Matthew and Luke include).

Himself as the Son of God. Mark attests to that frequently. Just look at Mark 1:1, 11; 3:1; 5:7; 9:7; 13:32; 14:61; and 15:39.

Luke

As we get to Luke's account of Jesus' life and ministry, we are able to slow down and catch our breath. Even though Luke has the same goal of presenting Jesus as the Anointed One of the Most High, he cautiously and deliberately aims the spotlight at Him. He begins his Gospel by carefully establishing his purpose for writing. It's the aim of this first century physician to present the human side of the divine Messiah. No wonder he gives the most complete account of Jesus' ancestry, birth, and child development. Luke alone provides us with a peek at Jesus as a pre-teen (2:41–52).

Just like we'd expect from a family doctor, Luke sensitively describes Jesus as One who reaches out personally and heals those who are mercilessly caged by devastating illnesses. As a person, He is concerned with people. Whereas Matthew likes to refer to Jesus as the Son of David and Mark refers to Him as the Son of God, Luke's favorite expression is "the Son of Man."

Jesus' humanity and compassion are repeatedly stressed by the author. This, coupled with Luke's portrayal of Jesus' sinless perfection, set up his logical conclusion. Because Jesus is the only perfect person born of a woman and because He identifies compassionately with the plight of suffering sinful people, He alone is qualified to carry our sorrows, bear our sin, and offer us the priceless gift of salvation. Did you get that? He died so we could claim His reputation. And even though we will never be perfect, Jesus' perfect example motivates us to follow His example and give others what they don't deserve.

John

In a manner of speaking, Jesus is the one-of-a-kind coin that purchased our redemption. But like any other coin, each side has a differing designation.

Whereas Luke wants us to see the human side of Jesus, the apostle John calls attention to the flip side. This beloved disciple shares an eyewitness account of what

In a manner of speaking, Jesus is the one-of-a-kind coin that purchased our redemption.

he experienced firsthand to convince us of Jesus' divine nature. And that side of the coin is in view from the first verse of the first chapter, where John introduces us to Jesus as the pre-existent Word of God and co-Creator of the universe.

The same side of the coin is visible when, near the end of his Gospel, John makes sure we understand the reason he is writing his account of Jesus' life. "These are written that you may believe that Jesus is the Christ, the Son of God and that believing you may have life in His name" (21:31).

John focuses on the claim that Jesus made that He was God by including Christ's seven "I am" statements: "I am the bread of life" (6:35, 48); "I am the light of the world" (8:12); "I am the door" (10:7, 9); "I am the good shepherd" (10:11, 14); "I am the resurrection and the life" (11:25); "I am the way, the truth and the life" (14:6); and "I am the true vine" (15:1–5).

John doesn't take any chances that we might miss

what these "I am" statements suggest. He records certain occasions when Jesus equates Himself with the Old Testament "I AM" (Yahweh). You can't be more specific than this: "Most assuredly, I say to you, before Abraham was, I AM" (8:58). But go ahead and discover for yourself who Jesus claimed to be in John 4:25–26; 8:24; 13:19; and 18:5–8.

Perhaps you are wondering if John believed in Jesus' divinity to the exclusion of His humanity. Wonder no longer. John notes that the Word was God, but also became flesh (1:14) He takes great pains to show us Jesus exhausted (4:6), thirsty (4:7), troubled (12:27), and dying (19:1–30).

.

CHAPTER SEVEN

Jesus in the Book of Acts

Acts

Biographies are written against the backdrop of history, culture, and people who were part of the subject's life. The Acts of the Apostles is such a backdrop. It offers a logical sequel to the four Gospels. In actuality it is Luke's continuation of the account he wrote of Jesus' life.

It is in the pages of Acts that we meet those who gave structure to the community of faith Jesus started. Even though it is called the Acts (or works) of the Apostles, it chronicles the experiences of more than those few. What we see in Acts is the ministry of the ascended and unseen Christ through the lives of ordinary people who make themselves available to Him. Don't believe it? Just look at how Dr. Luke begins his sequel.

"The former account I made, O Theophilus, of all that Jesus began both to do and teach . . ." (1:1). Luke is referring to his Gospel. But notice the word "began." The assumption is that Jesus is continuing His mission of redemption, healing, and love through those He commissioned. "You shall be my witnesses to me in Jerusalem, Judea and Samaria and to the end of the earth" (1:8).

Just because Jesus ascends into heaven in Chapter 1 doesn't mean He doesn't figure significantly into the rest of Acts.

Those are Jesus' last words on earth, and they set up what Luke lays out in the subsequent twenty-eight chapters with care and precision. Just because Jesus ascends into heaven in Chapter 1 doesn't mean He doesn't figure significantly into the rest of Acts. The resurrected Christ is the central theme of the sermons, defenses, and the life of the church through the entire book.

Luke intended Acts to be an apologetic that logically attests to Jesus' divinity. And he accomplished his purpose. Just look at the Old Testament Scriptures he cites. Notice his reference to the eyewitness accounts of Jesus' Resurrection, the firsthand testimonies of Jesus' followers (including a converted critic of Christianity by the name of Saul), and the evidence of the Holy Spirit's supernatural power. No wonder Luke quotes Peter as saying "To Him all the prophets witness that, through His name, whoever believes in Him will receive remission of sins" (10:43). "Nor is there salvation in any other, for there is no other name under heaven given among men by which we must be saved" (4:12).

CHAPTER EIGHT

Jesus in Paul's Epistles

Romans

In Luke's convincing account of the early church and its leaders, we are introduced to a reluctant disciple who encountered the risen Christ in a supernatural way. This educated rabbi who led a resistance movement, in which followers of Jesus were jailed and executed, had a Damascus Road experience . . . the very first on record. His name was changed from Saul to Paul.

Given Paul's initial defiance toward the message of Christ, it is remarkable that he would become the author of much of the New Testament. In his letter to the Christians in Rome, Paul pulls out all the stops to offer a systematic explanation of what Jesus' death means. The epistle to the Romans is logical as well as practical. The four Gospels present the words and works of Jesus, but this "Gospel" according to Paul is unique. It doesn't just convey facts to believe; it presents a life to be lived.

But what does he say about Jesus in his magnum opus? Well, for one thing, Paul explains that Jesus Christ is the Second Adam whose righteousness and substitutionary death have provided justification for all who place their faith in Him. Whew! Did you catch all that? If not, don't worry. By reading Romans you can see how the apostle breaks down that truckload of theological truth into bite-sized installments by using a question-and-answer format.

Perhaps a sample of what he writes would help to explain what he communicates about Jesus. "Therefore as through one man's offense judgment came to all men, resulting in condemnation, even so through one Man's righteous act the free gift came to all men resulting in justification of life. For as by one man's disobedience many were made sinners, so also by one Man's obedience, many will be made righteous" (5:18–19).

In other words, Romans presents a Jesus who offers His righteousness as a gracious gift to sinful people like us because He bore God's condemnation and wrath for our depraved nature. Paul makes it quite clear that the Savior's life, death, and Resurrection are the basis for our redemption, justification, reconciliation, salvation, and glorification. What is more, Paul contends that the Spirit of Jesus can motivate us to live responsible, Christlike lives. That's what the second half of Romans is all about.

1 Corinthians

It doesn't take a biblical scholar to see that each letter Paul writes has a distinct flavor. Whereas Romans dealt with doctrinal concerns, 1 Corinthians is aimed at helping a dysfunctional congregation discover its incredible potential. The apostle knows this church well. He planted it several years earlier. (See Acts 18:1–17.) He also knows it is perched for significant ministry in an important (yet godless) city of first-century Greece. But before it can be a cleansing agent in a corrupt community, this fellowship of Christ-followers needs to be purged of factions, lawsuits, and immorality.

But before it can be a cleansing agent in a corrupt community, this fellowship of Christ-followers needs to be purged of factions, lawsuits, and immorality.

That's where Paul's focus on 1 Corinthians comes into view. In this letter he proclaims the relevance of Christ Jesus to every area of the believer's life. In the writer's words, Jesus "became for us wisdom from

God—righteousness and sanctification and redemption" (1:30).

Paul goes on to assert (much like Luke did in Acts) that Jesus is living out His life in the world through the Church. According to Paul, we are the body of Christ with individual gifts. As we discover our gifts and invest them in mutual ministry, Jesus continues to touch the world for which He died (12:1–31).

2 Corinthians

After Paul wrote his first letter to the Christians in Corinth, critics of the apostle started sowing seeds of rebellion. Much of what Paul had written was being undermined by their false accusations. He pens this second installment to defend his conduct, character, and calling as an apostle of Christ. In this very intimate piece of correspondence, Paul is willing to be quite vulnerable. As a fresh reading of the text will reveal, he comes across quite Christlike. This is obviously true in his humility and also in what he suffered. "From the Jews five times I received forty stripes minus one. Three times I was beaten with rods; once I was stoned; three times I was shipwrecked . . ." (11:24–25).

Because Paul indicates he experienced the comfort of the risen Christ in the midst of his hardships, he reveals Jesus as the source of the believer's comfort. "For as the sufferings of Christ abound in us, so our consolation also abounds through Christ" (1:5).

Given Paul's personal tragedies, Jesus the Comforter is a major emphasis in this letter. But, look further and you will find much more. Jesus is celebrated as our triumph (2:14), our light (4:6), our reconciliation (5:19), our substitute (5:21), our gift (9:15), and our power (12:9).

But lest you think the apostle is less up front with the Corinthians about the holy nature of the risen Christ, Paul also reveals Jesus as our Lord (4:5), our judge (5:10), and our owner (10:7).

Galatians

Paul has been called by some New Testament scholars "the apostle of grace." The reason is clear. He knows our tendency to begin a walk with Christ down the path of faith only to take a rabbit trail into the wilderness of works. Paul's grace-ful emphasis comes through loud and clear in his letter to the Christians in Galatia. His vigorous attack against their "gospel according to good works" begins with a review of his conversion and his credentials.

Paul introduces Jesus to this errant flock as the One

in whom the message of grace is grounded. "For I neither received it from man nor was I taught it, but it came through the revelation of Jesus Christ" (1:12).

He's suspended our license to do whatever we want. Instead Jesus has created an environment where we breathe the oxygen of liberty and have the power to do what we ought.

It's a message declaring that Jesus has freed the Christian from the bondage to the law. Legalism is no longer a master to whom we are accountable. It is this same Jesus who has set the believer free from sin. He's suspended our license to do whatever we want. Instead Jesus has created an environment where we breathe the oxygen of liberty and have the power to do what we ought.

The Jesus whom Paul encountered en route to Syria has reversed the curse of sin, law, and self. (See 1:4; 2:20; 3:13; 4:5; 5:24; and 6:14.) What makes this reversal possible is nothing other than the transforming power of the Cross.

Ephesians

Unlike the Galatians, the Christians who lived in and around Ephesus were not blind to the grace of God. But they did suffer from an eye disorder. They were an unbelievably wealthy congregation (spiritually speaking), but they were somehow unable to focus on their inheritance.

Paul writes his epistle to the Ephesians challenging them to quit living like beggars and open their eyes to the resources God had given them. The inheritance is what Jesus, their divine Benefactor, had bequeathed them. And throughout his letter Paul continues to reference Jesus.

The phrase "in Christ" (or its equivalent) appears about thirty-five times. Without a doubt that's more than any other book in the New Testament. Jesus is not a distant stone deity like the pagan goddess Diana (whose magnificent temple towered over Ephesus). Jesus is alive and empowered as the Lord of all creation. He is seated at the right hand of God's throne where He interacts with His followers on earth in a dynamic way. Jesus, says Paul, is "head over all things to the church, which is His body, the fullness of Him who fills all in all" (1:22–23).

Just imagine the supernatural power this entitles us to. We are in Christ, having been personally chosen by Him (1:4). And we are seated in the heavenly places in Him (1:3). That sounds a bit ethereal, doesn't it? But it isn't just a charming idea; it's the promise of hope.

Paul's point is that in Jesus we've been given hope (1:12) and made alive (2:5) in order to grow (2:21) and make a difference in this world by the way we live. "For by grace you have been saved through faith, and that not of yourselves, it is the gift of God. . . . For we are His workmanship, created in Christ Jesus for good works which God prepared beforehand that we should walk in them" (2:8–9).

Philippians

If it's beginning to sound like the Christian life is inseparable from the life of the risen Christ, you're catching on to Paul's core doctrine. Jesus' presence overshadows all the Christian thinks and attempts. And because of that, Christians are to be mindful of how they behave. There is no excuse for self-centeredness or divisions in the church.

The Christians in Philippi didn't have a very firm grasp on that concept. Although they were helpful to Paul during a season when he experienced much suffering, they needed to be reminded that Jesus demanded full commitment. In the same letter in which he thanks them for their help, Paul calls to mind that the Son of God is to be their standard of comparison when it comes to a surrendered life.

Paul picks up his pen and (as if brushing a canvas) paints several portraits of the Savior. In Chapter 1 the apostle reveals that Christ's life cannot be distinguished from His followers'. "For me to live is Christ" (1:21). In Chapter 2 he frames a humble profile of Jesus by picturing Him as the model of true humility. "Let this mind be in you which was also in Christ Jesus . . ." (2:5). Paul continues to paint. In Chapter 3 he presents Jesus as the One who alone is capable of transforming our lowly bodies that they might be conformed to His glorious body (3:21).

> *The apostle reveals that Christ's life cannot be distinguished from His followers'. "For me to live is Christ.*

But it is the ever-popular fourth chapter where Paul hangs his own self-portrait, which extols Jesus' power that has carried him through difficult circumstances over and over again. Along with the apostle, we can also claim, "I can do all things through Christ who strengthens me" (4:13).

Colossians

Philippians isn't the only letter Paul writes from behind bars. Evidence points to the fact that Ephesians was penned while the apostle was incarcerated, too. So was Colossians. But Paul's whereabouts when he wrote this letter pale in significance to what he has to say. If Ephesians can be labeled the epistle of the church of Christ, then Colossians must be the epistle about the Christ of the church. As someone has graphically described, Ephesians focuses on the Body. Colossians takes aim at the Head.

Thanks to Paul, Colossians is the one book in the New Testament that uniquely centers on the cosmic Christ—the head of all the "principalities and powers" (2:10). But it is more than just that. Paul wants us to know that in Jesus we see the face of God. "He is the image of the invisible God" (1:15). As such, Jesus' divine nature and Incarnation are celebrated by the apostle as watershed realities. Paul doesn't want that awesome concept to cause our heads to spin, so he spends the rest of the letter helping us understand what all that means in our lives.

This image of the invisible God is the Author of reconciliation (1:20–22; 2:13–15) and our Redeemer and Reconciler (2:11–15, 20–22). Because that is a given, it only stands to reason that He is the basis for all believers' hope (1:5, 23, 27).

Paul has a tendency to wax theological, but even

without a seminary degree you can walk away from
Colossians fully convinced that Jesus is the resurrected
God–man (2:18; 3:1) who continues
to be our Creator and Sustainer
(1:16–17). He remains the Head of
the church and in that role is all-
sufficient (1:18, 28).

> *Paul wants
> us to know
> that in Jesus
> we see the
> face of God.
> "He is the
> image of the
> invisible
> God."*

1 Thessalonians

The self-sufficiency of Christ is
more than a doctrine to Paul. What
he postulates in his letter to the believers in Colosse
is being lived out by the church in Thessalonica.
The faith, hope, love, and perseverance of the young
church Paul started is exemplary. As a proud parent
he beams with pride. His father-like devotion has
been rewarded.

But the apostle knows that the laws of entropy
work their woes in congregations just like in individuals. Untended fires burn out. Paul writes to his friends
to encourage them. And he does that by pointing
them to Jesus. "We urge and exhort in the Lord Jesus
that you should abound more and more, just as you
received from us how you ought to walk and to please

God. For you know what commandments we gave you through the Lord Jesus" (4:1–2).

Not only does Paul encourage the Thessalonians, but he also motivates their faithfulness by alluding to Jesus' Second Coming. Jesus is pictured in this letter as the believers' hope of salvation both now and when He returns to earth. At that time He will deliver us from the wrath that will envelop the world (1:10; 5:4–11). This same Jesus will reward our faithfulness with His physical presence (2:19) after He has resurrected our mortal bodies. "For the Lord Himself will descend from heaven. . . . We who are alive and remain shall be caught up together. . . . And thus we shall always be with the Lord" (4:13–18).

In the meantime Paul reminds them (and us) that Jesus is committed to our spiritual growth. "And may the Lord make you increase and abound in love" (3:12). Even maturing Christians like these in Thessalonica need help in that regard.

2 Thessalonians

What was that about atrophy? It seems the fervor of the Thessalonians did begin to flag. Since Paul's first letter arrived, the seeds of false doctrine had been sown among members of this congregation. It caused them to waver in their commitment. Somehow the church was led to believe the day of Jesus' return had already passed.

If that were true, why would you hold to a disciplined life? Why labor diligently for the sake of the gospel? These are questions Paul must address. Paul writes a second letter in an attempt to weed out the erroneous teaching in their midst.

For the apostle the answer is an easy one. The day of the Lord has not come and gone. Jesus' return is still pending. As in his first letter, Paul presents Jesus as the joyful hope of all Christians. His eventual return will more than make up for the persecution, suffering, and injustices we are currently anticipating or enduring.

His eventual return will more than make up for the persecution, suffering, and injustices we are currently anticipating or enduring.

In case you're wondering, the return of Jesus is mentioned in the New Testament more than any other doctrine—318 times, to be exact. When that final day comes, everything promised in Scripture will be fulfilled. No wonder Paul spends the first two chapters of 2 Thessalonians consumed with the topic.

Although the Lord's presence will be worth it all

for those who look for Him with hope, His return
has awesome and terrifying implications for those who
refuse to trust in His salvation (1:6–10; 2:8–12).

1 Timothy

One young disciple who trusted in Jesus' sacrifice
early on in his life was Timothy. We don't know
anything about his father, but his mother and grand-
mother successfully passed the baton of faith to him.
As a young adult Timothy became the pastor of the
church in Ephesus. Though mature in his faith, he is
overwhelmed by the challenges in the congregation.
False doctrine must be erased, public worship must
be safeguarded, and responsible godly leaders must
be developed.

Paul writes to Timothy to encourage him and to
instruct him to guard himself as well as the congregation from sin. In his words we see Jesus' approach to
disciple-making. Although Paul was not one of the
original twelve, his consistent investment in Timothy
mirrors that of the Master mentor.

In this letter Paul presents Jesus as "the one mediator between God and man" (2:5). But don't think
the apostle is backing away from his belief in the full
divinity of Jesus. In the very next chapter he reminds

his young apprentice that "God was manifested in the flesh, justified in the Spirit, seen by angels, preached among the Gentiles, believed on in the world and received up in glory" (3:16).

Whew! And that's not all. The reason Jesus came to earth was to save sinners (1:15) by giving Himself as a ransom for all (2:6). Paul wants Timothy to know that this One who is both God and man not only has our salvation in mind but is also the source of spiritual strength, faith, and love (1:12, 14). No wonder the apostle wants Timothy to focus on Jesus as he faces the challenges of ministry. Jesus is the Savior in every and all circumstances (4:10).

2 Timothy

You can't help but see Jesus in Paul. His devotion to this young friend does not decline even when the aged apostle is facing death. What Jesus modeled in loving His disciples to the end, Paul maintains toward Timothy. He writes this second letter to Timothy to assure him of his prayers and love. He does this by referring to the young pastor's spiritual heritage. He communicates his belief in Timothy's abilities by making demands on him that will push him to excellence.

They are demands that can only be met by continually looking to Jesus.

In this follow-up correspondence, Paul identifies Christ Jesus as the One who appeared on earth in order to abolish death and bring life and immortality to light (1:10). The apostle reminds Timothy that Jesus was the fulfillment of God's promises to David and that He validated His mission by conquering death

The apostle reminds Timothy that Jesus was the fulfillment of God's promises to David and that He validated His mission by conquering death.

(2:8). But Paul is candid enough to move beyond the creedal affirmations of faith to speak about the personal consequences of following the Son of God. "All who desire to live godly in Christ Jesus will suffer persecution" (3:12).

In this little epistle, Jesus is nothing less than the source of our salvation, our faith, and the gospel we proclaim, which will surely make waves in the world. No wonder Paul writes to Timothy to inspire perseverance. Conflict and resistance come with the turf of discipleship. But Paul the motivator par excellence looks to the end of the race and reminds his friend that all who love Jesus' appearing will receive the crown of righteousness (4:8). Even more, they will one day reign with Christ (2:12).

Titus

Paul's heart for young pastors beats nonstop. He reached out to Timothy, and now he is reaching out to Titus. Just as Timothy did, Titus also finds himself in over his head. The congregation on the island of Crete lacked organization and structure. Paul knows what's needed and writes this letter.

You can't help but appreciate how Paul fleshes out Jesus' style of leadership development.

The wrinkled and worn out apostle instructs Titus to appoint godly elders to oversee the work of the church. But he also challenges this younger pastor to call the entire congregation to a lifestyle like Jesus'. You can't help but appreciate how Paul fleshes out Jesus' style of leadership development. What the Savior did on boat rides in Galilee or on hikes through the Jordan Valley, Paul does with his pen.

The implication that can be drawn from this is easy to identify. Any letter Paul writes is going to have the fragrance of his Lord. That's one way we see Jesus in this tiny letter. But there is more.

As in others of Paul's letters, his greeting refers to the grace, mercy, and peace that are available from both God the Father and the Lord Jesus Christ (1:4). And the reason Paul refers to them as a unit is because of his unflappable belief that Jesus is one with the Father. In Titus 2:13 he refers to Him as our great God and Savior. Obviously that is not unique to this letter, but it is noteworthy. So is the way Paul calls attention to Jesus being the "blessed hope" who has yet to return to earth for those for whom He died (2:13).

And speaking of Jesus' death, just savor Paul's beautiful description of the Savior's redemptive work on our behalf: "who gave Himself for us that He might redeem us from every lawless deed and purify for Himself His own special people, zealous for good works" (2:14). Certainly Titus got the message.

Philemon

Not all who benefited from Paul's personal friendship and instruction were congregations or young pastors. One person in particular is a runaway slave. His name is Onesimus. We learn about him in this postcard-sized epistle Paul wrote to his friend Philemon.

Onesimus at one time worked for Philemon, a leader in the Colossian church. But the slave robbed his master and ran away to Rome. While there, Onesimus encounters Paul, and through the apostle's influence, he encounters Christ. Herein lies the dilemma and the purpose of this little letter.

Onesimus, the new convert, has become a new creature in Christ and has become extremely valuable to Paul. But both of them know that Onesimus has a moral obligation as a Christian to return to Philemon. It is what Paul pens in this passionate letter (that the ex-slave will personally carry to Philemon) that we "see" Jesus in this book.

The forgiveness that the believer finds in Christ is beautifully portrayed by analogy. Although Onesimus is guilty of a great offense (vv. 11, 18), Paul is moved to intercede on his behalf. Paul lays asides his rights (v. 8) and becomes Onesimus's substitute by assuming his debt (vv. 18–19). That's what Jesus did for Paul, and for every one of us. By Philemon's gracious act, Onesimus will be restored and placed in a new relationship (vv. 15–16). In this analogy, we are like Onesimus, while Paul's advocacy before Philemon is parallel to Christ's work of mediation before the Father.

CHAPTER NINE

Jesus in the General Epistles

Hebrews

Reading only up to this point, one might think that Paul was the only Christian leader capable of carrying on correspondence with churches in the first century. Not so! Peter, John, James, and others were quite confident with a quill and an ink pot, too. What they do find difficult to do, however, is to write a letter without any inference or direct mention of the One in whose name they write. They can't get their minds off Jesus.

Although the identity of the author of Hebrews is difficult to trace, his message is quite easy to follow. Many Jewish believers, having stepped out of Judaism into Christianity, wanted to reverse their course in order to escape persecution from their countrymen. But the writer stops them in their tracks, exhorting them to "go on to perfection" (6:1). His appeal is based on the superiority of Christ. The Judaic system of sacrifice and priestly rule pales in comparison to Christ's work. The writer insists that Jesus is better than the angels, for even the angels worship Him (2:5). Jesus is better than Moses, for He created him (3:3). Jesus is better than the Aaronic priesthood, for His sacrifice was once for all time (5:4). And He is better than the law, for He mediates a better covenant.

In a book that is earmarked for a Jewish audience (much like the Gospel of Matthew is), the author presents Jesus as the divine-human Prophet, Priest, and King.

The author obviously is appealing to those with a Jewish background. He keeps referring to the Old Testament. For example, he says that Jesus is our eternal High Priest according to the order of Melchizedek (5:6, 10). What is more, He identifies with us in His Incarnation and offers no less a sacrifice than Himself on our behalf. In a book that is earmarked for a Jewish audience (much like the Gospel of Matthew is), the author presents Jesus as the divine-human Prophet, Priest, and King. As you read through the book, you can see that His deity (1:1–3, 8) and humanity (2:9, 14, 17, 18) are asserted with equal force. More than twenty titles are used to describe His attributes and accomplishments (e.g., Heir of all things, apostle and High Priest, Mediator, Author, and Perfecter of Faith). And the bottom line is unmistakable. Jesus is superior to all who went before and offers the supreme sacrifice, priesthood, and covenant.

James

Paul, the apostle of grace, successfully planted several churches. His message of salvation through faith alone countered the prevalent view that acceptance by God was conditioned by keeping the Jewish law. Understandably, those who struggled (without success) to obey the Jewish laws were only too glad to let go of the legalistic demands of Moses once they accepted Christ.

The problem came when some of the converted Jews threw the baby out with the bath water. Hadn't Jesus said He came to fulfill the law, not destroy it (Matthew 5:17)? Enter James, the half-brother of Jesus. Here is a man who accepted his Brother's messianic identity somewhat reluctantly. But once he believed, he believed with all his heart.

James writes his epistle to the twelve tribes of Israel that are scattered around the first-century world. His passion is to put Christian practice in its proper place.

Faith, observes James, is well and good, but "faith by itself, if it does not have works, is dead" (2:17).

Compared to New Testament writers, James says little about Jesus. He begins his book referring to the Lord Jesus Christ (1:1; 2:1) and anticipates "the coming of the Lord" (5:7), but that's about it in terms of direct references. Still, James' message is virtually saturated in Jesus' teachings. The Sermon on the Mount in particular figures prominently into James' thinking. If you stop and count them, you'll find the author making indirect reference to that most famous of all sermons multiple times. (James 1:2 is based on Matthew 5:10–12. James 1:4 is connected to Matthew 5:48. James 2:13 relates to Matthew 6:14–15. James 4:11 relates to Matthew 7:1–2. And James 5:2 is understood in light of Matthew 6:13.)

Through his teaching, James presents Jesus as One who insists that the righteous of His followers exceed that of the Pharisees (Matthew 5:20).

1 Peter

Obviously James understood Jesus, having known Him for years prior to His public ministry. The apostle Peter, on the other hand, got to know the Lord in a very different way, through an extensive, three-and-a-half year period of on-the-job training.

Peter witnessed his Lord's suffering firsthand. He suffered in his own way when he was caught in his cowardly betrayal of Jesus. The Savior predicted Peter's indiscretion, but He also predicted that Peter would taste the bitter pill of persecution years later.

God laid it on Peter's heart to write an epistle to Jewish believers who are exiled and enduring hardship because of their faith in Jesus. Writing to encourage them, Peter succeeds in boosting their perseverance quotient. He presents Jesus as the believers' supreme example and hope in times of suffering in a hostile world. "If Jesus could do it, by His strength, you can, too!"

He presents Jesus as the believers' supreme example and hope in times of suffering in a hostile world.

For Peter, Jesus is the basis for our living hope and inheritance (1:3–4). What is more, the love relationship that is available with Him is a source of inexpressible joy (1:8). Peter is quick to convey what Paul and the Gospel writers have already established, that Jesus' suffering and death provide redemption for all who trust in Him "who Himself bore our sins in His own body on the tree, that we, having died to sins, might live for righteousness—by whose stripes you were healed" (2:24).

Jesus also is lifted up as the Chief Shepherd and Overseer of all Christians (2:25; 5:4), and when He appears, those who have a relationship with Him will be glorified.

2 Peter

Not all the suffering that Christians face is at the hands of persecutors outside the church walls. Sometimes the cause for concern is within the sanctuary. Peter writes this second letter to Christians scattered hither and yon to warn them about false teachers peddling dangerous doctrine who have infiltrated their gatherings. The apostle calls them to be on their guard against such counterfeit Christians.

But he also calls them to keep close watch on their personal lives. Wrong attitudes and behavior can be just as damaging as wrong beliefs. As in his first epistle, Peter points to Jesus as the means by which our inner lives can remain godly. The Lord Jesus Christ, he says, is the source of full knowledge and power for the attainment of spiritual maturity (1:2, 3, 8; 3:18). Peter recalls the glory of Jesus' transfiguration on the holy mountain. He should know. He was there. And upon reflection upon that unforgettable experience, Peter anticipates the Lord's glorious return to earth. Then it won't just be three men on a mountain who see Him. All will behold His glory.

1 John

Isn't it good to know God cares about those who need to be encouraged? The letters of Peter were not written to individual churches. They were written to believers who were homeless, uprooted, and discouraged. In much the same way, the apostle John writes the first of his three brief letters to Christians-at-large, who need to be reminded that God's incarnation in the form of His Son Jesus was not only spiritual but physical as well.

A heretical movement known as Gnosticism was gaining in popularity. It denied that Jesus really did have a human body. In an attempt to battle such nonsense, the apostle goes straight for the jugular. Jesus was both divine

John is not only concerned with countering the Gnostics' claims. He also desires to encourage the persecuted believers by reminding them of Jesus' present ministry among them.

and human. In the very first verses, John attests to what he has experienced personally. "That which was from the beginning, which we have heard, which we have seen with our eyes, which we have looked upon, and our hands have handled, concerning the Word of Life—the life was manifested, and we have seen and bear witness and declare to you that eternal life which was with the Father and was manifested to us" (1:1–2).

But John is not only concerned with countering the Gnostics' claims. He also desires to encourage the persecuted believers by reminding them of Jesus' present ministry among them. It's portrayed in 1:5—2:22. The Savior's blood continually cleanses us from all sin. That's because, as John emphasizes, Jesus is our righteous Advocate before the Father.

2 John

Because 1 John is a letter without an address, we aren't sure who the first recipients were. In his second letter we do know. John writes "to the elect lady and her children" (v. 1). We don't presume to know exactly who they are. Some suggest it is a code name to protect a persecuted individual or congregation. We can surmise, however, that the recipients were facing the same threats of Gnosticism as those in 1 John.

Once again John takes sharp aim at these who deny the bodily reality of Jesus. The Jesus of whom he writes (and whom he knows intimately) had flesh and blood and bones. He labels the insurrectionists as false teachers. And whereas John often proclaims the message to "love one another," he forcefully demands that Christians have nothing to do with heretics such as these. "For many deceivers have gone out into the world who do not confess Jesus Christ as coming in the flesh . . . do not receive him into your house nor greet him" (vv. 7, 10).

Why would you think John is so adamant? The reason is obvious. In order to have a relationship with God the Father, you must abide "in the doctrine of Christ" the Son (v. 9). You cannot approach the Father without going through Jesus. For John, the person and work of Jesus Christ affect every area of life and faith.

3 John

In his first epistle, John celebrates the Incarnation of Jesus and the fellowship with God that "the Word made flesh" makes possible. In his second little epistle, he forbids fellowship with those who deny the reality of the Incarnation. In his third piece of correspondence, the apostle encourages fellowship among Christians.

Unlike his first two letters, John doesn't mention Jesus' name at all in this last one. However, before you go jumping to false conclusions, you'll want to take note of verse 7.

Here John is referring to a group of itinerant Christian missionaries. They are ministering "for His name's sake." That, to be sure, is an indirect reference to Jesus. We can figure that out by looking back to the fifth chapter of Acts. There we read the account of how John himself and several others were beaten by the Jewish council and commanded not to speak in Jesus' name. But, as the text relates, the apostles were not intimidated. Upon release they rejoiced "that they were counted worthy to suffer shame for His name" (5:41). Whose name? Obviously, Jesus' name.

So John does reference the Savior in this third letter after all. Jesus is the means and motivation for taking the Good News to the world. That is, after all, why these missionaries were on the move and in need of Christian hospitality and fellowship. Without such, they would have no place to stay.

Jude

Wise old Solomon is credited with writing the famous words that a music group called The Byrds recorded in the 1970s. "For every time there is a season . . . a time to love and a time to hate. . . ."

Well, Jude's little one-chapter letter is about a time to hate. He jolts his readers to attention by calling Christians to fight, contend, and do battle. He is keenly aware that when the truth of God is attacked, the faith must be defended.

Those churches to whom Jude writes had been infiltrated by pleasure-seeking teachers who had transformed grace into a sensual license. Grace was being perverted into a permission slip for irresponsible and ungodly living. With the authority and ring of a military general, he gives specific orders to remember the words of Jesus' apostles to build themselves up in the faith (v. 20) and to keep themselves in the love of God (v. 21).

Grace was being perverted into a permission slip for irresponsible and ungodly living. With the authority and ring of a military general, he gives specific orders to remember the words of Jesus' apostles.

But just how are they to go about doing that? He answers what our inquisitive minds want to know, that the key is to keep "looking for the mercy of our Lord Jesus Christ unto eternal life" (v. 21). Whereas those who follow immoral desires and deny Christ will be condemned, Jude assures believers that Jesus is the One who preserves us and keeps us. In fact, the beginning and ending of his letter celebrate this assuring reality. The letter is addressed "to those who are preserved in Jesus Christ" (v. 1) and closes with praise "to Him who is able to keep you from stumbling and to present you faultless before the presence of His glory with exceeding joy, to God our Savior" (vv. 24–25). What a blessed assurance that Christ holds us close; He never fails.

CHAPTER TEN

Jesus in Revelation

Revelation

The Bible is a one-volume library. In it are biographies, a hymnal, poetry books, a love story, chronicles of war and history, and a collection of personal letters. If you were to have to choose one category of which all the other categories would be sub-sets, you'd no doubt choose "history." But you wouldn't spell it the traditional way. It would be spelled "His Story."

Jesus, the Word of God is found on almost every page in the Scripture in one way or another. In the final book of the Bible, the risen Christ doesn't settle for a bit part. He is the spotlighted Actor on stage, front and center.

In the mysteriously wonderful letter we call Revelation, the exiled apostle John, wrinkled by age and weary from decades of faithful ministry, transcribes a vision he had

In this three-dimensional Technicolor vision, the risen and ascended Christ offers a prophetic word to the seven churches and a glimpse of the future for Christians everywhere.

on the island of Patmos. In this three-dimensional Technicolor vision, the risen and ascended Christ offers a prophetic word to the seven churches and a glimpse of the future for Christians everywhere.

One thing the author conveys about Jesus is that He continues to lead and interact with His church. In addition, He alone has received authority to judge the earth. Just note the terms John uses to refer to Jesus: He is called Jesus Christ (1:1), the faithful Witness, the Firstborn from the dead, the Ruler over the kings of the earth (1:5), the First and the Last (1:17), He who lives (1:18), the Son of God (2:18), holy and true (3:7), the Amen, the Faithful and True Witness, the Beginning of the creation of God (3:14), the Lion of the tribe of Judah, the Root of David (5:5), a Lamb (5:6), Faithful and True (19:11), the Word of God (19:13), KING OF KINGS AND LORD OF LORDS (19:16), Alpha and Omega (22:13), the Bright and Morning Star (22:16), and the Lord Jesus Christ (22:21).

This eerie and awesome "letter" to the universal church comes from Him and centers on Him. It begins with a vision of His glory, wisdom, and power (ch. 1) and portrays His authority over the entire church (2:3). He is the Lamb who was slain and declared worthy to open the book of judgment (ch. 5). It is this same Jesus who will pour out His righteous wrath on the whole earth (ch. 6—18). It is this same Jesus who will return in power to judge His enemies and to reign as the Lord over all forever (19:20).

No wonder this last book of the Bible is called The Revelation of Jesus Christ.